Steps in the Middle

The thorn under my feet...
and when the pain didn't matter anymore...

Ernest Mhande

Steps in the Middle
The thorn under my feet...
and when the pain didn't matter anymore...

© 2017 Publisher
All rights reserved

ISBN- 978-0-9953614-2-3

No part of this book may be reproduced by any mechanical,
photographic or electronic process, nor stored in any retrieval system,
transmitted, translated into another language, or otherwise copied for
public or private use, excepting brief passages quoted
for purposes of review, without the express written
permission of the publisher

Acknowledgements

I am grateful to several people for their insights, criticisms and encouraging words, leading to, and during, the work on this story.

I would like to express my gratitude to my family including Walter who stuck with me during the process and kept my hopes alive even when it was difficult. I am grateful to all my friends and colleagues for reading my manuscripts and providing me with invaluable suggestions of expressing the story. The graphics including the page layout and cover design were provided by Reality Premedia Services. I am grateful that they understood my intentions, presented my words and ideas very well.

Thank you.

Contents

1. The marriage, the resolution and the New Job 1
2. The Family, the relocation and the Penrith Market 15
3. The army truck and Gabriel's death 27
4. The promise that never was 37
5. The trip back to her childhood home 47
6. When all that was left is lost 61
7. The hen gathers all her chicks again 73
8. The road from St. Columbus 87
9. The day they knew who they were 95
10. The ambition and the self-discovery 113
11. Teaching manners and charity at home 119
12. Standing up for yourself when no one is available 139
13. Life principles, a dysfunctional home and keeping the focus.... 147
14. The mentors and the trip to Penrith 161
15. The mentor like no other 177
16. Self –discovery and misconceptions challenged 197
17. Love, dedication and self-sacrifice 207
18. One option is left, it's painful and there is no choice 221
19. Step through painful moments-can't be hurried 235
20. The ascend from the valley 251

CHAPTER 1

The marriage, the resolution and the New Job

A few yards from the house were two tall trees, easily visible from a distance. As the spring season gave way to winter, the leaves turned yellow before falling off the trees. When the wind blew, some leaves fell on rooftops of nearby houses and those too would be blown away landing around the house. The leaves covered the ground like a carpet. Then, as the season changed, new leaves, fresh and green, clothed the tree and a fresh scent ushered new life to the tree. Soon the trees were adorned with flowers; the blossoming flowers attracted the birds and bees. The coming of spring seemed to create a new excitement for both plants and animals.

The houses, a few steps away, had been constructed many years ago. Larry had erected two additional outbuildings in a disorganized fashion. Standards for housing construction at the time were non-existent. Larry remembered as vividly as yesterday when the builders first put up his house. During this period building material had to be sourced from Newcastle, a distance of over hundred miles away. Penrith was still a growing town, and not many supplies were available.

To the west of his homestead lay Larry's cornfields which had been harvested a few months earlier. Cattle, horses, and sheep were busy foraging on what was left in the fields. To the east of his estate were a thick forest and a path through the woods led to the village. Visitors to Larry's homestead coming from the eastern side of the estate were not easy to spot until they were very close. To the south of the house were paddocks leading into the hill nearby. The hill shielded Larry's house from the view of the mighty Cherwell River, which divided the village in half, running from east to west. It was a perennial source of water for the residents. Cattle, horses, and sheep grazed along the river banks during winter and autumn months in the days before Penrith grew into a town.

Every summer the river would come down in flood, cutting off access and communication between people on both sides of the river for days at a time. The flooding prevented anyone on the South from getting to the market and the children from attending school. It had taken many years before the authorities constructed a bridge to enable the people to cross the river safely, perhaps because there were so few families living across the river. The land south of the river comprised mainly of red and rocky loam soils, forming a slippery terrain that led into a dense forest which covered the mountain slopes.

The forest was also a source of timber and fruits. It provided grazing for cattle, horses, and sheep during difficult seasons. The livestock would be driven into the forest every morning and herded back to their paddocks before dusk. For many years, the villagers were able to leave their livestock unattended. However, the situation began to change with the civil war fast approaching. When the war started, Penrith was not directly affected by the hostilities which were still some distance away. However, as the years progressed, the fighting became closer. The noise of heavy machine gun and artillery fire was frequently heard from all directions and opposing army troops could be seen crisscrossing Penrith, although no actual fighting had been reported around Penrith.

Gabriel had met Maria five years earlier in Roselle when she was visiting her aunt who lived next to St Paul's mission. After knowing each other for a relatively short period, the two got married and started a family. The couple built their home about five miles west of St Pauls Mission and a walking distance from Gabriel's parents. Gabriel had no formal employment and like the rest of his brothers had no formal education. Every morning he would move from one place to another in search of casual jobs, and for years this was his sole source of income. His life, like that of his brothers, was a struggle in a community where a man's worth was measured by how well he provided for his family. Wealthy men of his day possessed large tracts of fertile land and livestock which could readily be sold for cash. Rich people were able to hire many hands to work at home and in the fields.

As was his routine, Gabriel woke up early and walked down the village in search of casual jobs. On his face was a troubled look; he was worried about the future of his two young children. All at once he was overwhelmed by a new determination to change his way of life. "I am poor, and if I don't work hard to change this, poverty will begin to inflict on my children," Gabriel spoke the words aloud as he walked down the village. "It is my responsibility to remove the curse of poverty from myself and my children, and I am going to do it," he shouted loudly in the early morning gloom and his words, if anyone was listening, echoed to the hills a short distance away to the east. "I have wept from time to time because of my situation, but now it is time for me to stop. I must decide what to do and take the necessary action," he spoke aloud again.

In his heart was a new resolve and a determination to extricate himself and his family from the shackles of poverty, which had mercilessly gripped his extended family from one generation to another. Just like other villagers, Gabriel had been in denial for years, attributing his life situation to the curse of the gods and misfortune. He had seen how his brothers continued to wallow in poverty from day to day, oblivious to their status. They neither cared about the gods nor their poverty as long as they had a meal for the day. "Perhaps, they are right to think that way, because at the end of everyone's life await death. So there may be no wisdom to amass many things, but what is wrong with accumulating wealth, if you can? Wouldn't it be better to die wealth than to die poor? If one can do better in life why can't they go ahead and be who they want to be? Should I be worried about working hard because of fear of my brothers? I have noticed everything worthwhile comes from an idea and taking action on the plan, and I have been searching for ideas day and night." Gabriel continued talking as he hurried down the village.

The villagers in Roselle endured crushing poverty on a daily basis – most families struggled to put food on the table. Agriculture was the primary source of livelihood while pests, weather, and excessive rains adversely affected crop yields. Even in good years, the sandy soils of Roselle did not produce good crops and rarely did villagers enjoy the surplus food. The on-going civil war placed livestock in cross-fire worsening the plight of villagers. The loss of cattle, their primary source of income, had a significant impact on their wealth and social standing.

Roselle primary school, just a stone's throw away, was nearly empty. One would have assumed that when education was free attendance rates would be high, but alas, Roselle primary school barely attained full attendance. Even though schooling was free, parents were required to pay a school levy to keep the school well-maintained, as was the case at other schools in the area. The amount required per child soon became a burden for many parents, and increasingly children began to miss school, not only for that reason but also because they were needed as casual labour to work alongside their parents in the fields. Working on the farms along with one's children seemed a quicker way of increasing income.

The sun was setting when Gabriel finished his assigned piece of work for the day. He had just been paid five dollars, the going rate for a day's wage at the time. He knew he had to look for another assignment the next day. He stood up, glanced at the sunset, picked up his farm tools and headed home. He was tired, and his muscles were aching. His empty stomach was groaning with hunger. Throughout the day the hot summer sun caused him heat rush and profuse sweating; now the sweat was drying as a cold breeze swept through from east to west. He dragged his feet wearily on the way home. As the sun set, birds were returning to their nests, cattle and horses were being secured in their enclosures. Soon, the hustle and bustle of the day were overtaken slowly by a peaceful evening.

As Gabriel approached his house, Mark and Martha, who were out waiting for their father, came running toward him. He quickened his steps toward his children, leaned down, picked them both up and kissed them. Then he placed them back on their feet again and together they walked to the house hand in hand. Gabriel cast his eyes toward his house and saw a man seated on a chair outside the house. He looked closely at the man again and suddenly realized that it was his uncle, Larry. Several thoughts crossed his mind. He pondered for moments as he drew closer to the house. "Uncle Larry! I wasn't expecting you," he exclaimed.

Larry regularly visited Roselle, but a year had passed since he last stayed over in Roselle. The last time he stayed over in Roselle was when he came to attend Joshua's burial and ever since that time, his visits had become very short. Larry and Joshua were close brothers who always regularly visited each other. Joshua died after a brief illness at home, and since then Larry had been to Roselle a number times to attend many family feuds. Larry had already moved from Roselle to Penrith ten years earlier. A few months before Joshua's death, Larry and Joshua had agreed that whoever would still be alive at the passing of the other, would look after the family of the fallen one. "Is there a problem?" Gabriel wondered. Gabriel welcomed Larry's trips to Roselle as it was his uncle's practice to bring some gifts, delicacies and fresh produce for his grandchildren to enjoy a good meal with him; this time was no different.

A delicious smell was pouring out of the kitchen where Maria was already preparing dinner for the family. She was good with roast beef, and as expected she wasted no time in cooking the meat Larry had brought. She boiled the meat for a few minutes in salt, pepper, and some herbs before grilling it on hot coals. The smell of burning fat dripping onto the hot coals wafted out of the kitchen. Even their two dogs struggled impatiently to wait for their portion of the meal.

Gabriel and Larry shook hands and sat side-by-side to talk. Larry looked at his nephew with concern; he could see that he was tired out from his field work. "How is the job situation these days?" he asked. "It's difficult to find a job; I can go for days at a time without a job. This very morning, I was thinking about the future of my children, and I realized how I needed to work hard, and do everything I can to improve my situation," Gabriel replied enthusiastically. "I am not going to have my children die of hunger nor am I going to be poor again." Larry was rather taken aback by Gabriel's response. Here was a man worn out by back breaking work yet speaking with energy and passion. His reaction wasn't the kind of enthusiasm Larry expected from a man at the end of a day's punishing work. Gabriel hadn't spoken to Larry like this before, and he seemed to have discovered a secret to life and a strong sense of urgency. "Have you found a new job then?" Larry asked. "No, uncle, it's just my thoughts that have changed. I have come to the conclusion that if I need my life to change, I should be the one to change my ways first. I can't continue to live and think like I did yesterday. I have new ideas on how to improve my life. From today, I am no longer going to wait for the gods to bring good fortune my way. I am going to go after my fortune, work hard day and night, and save a portion of my earnings so that I can pay for my children's education when they get to a school-going age," Gabriel replied. "I must heed the wisdom of those who have already achieved success. It is time to stop complaining about my lot in life and to do something about it," he continued. "Over the years, several wise and successful people have tried to help me with advice, but I have not been receptive to anyone financially better than me. I always argued with them and accused them of not understanding what it means to be poor. Today,

I have realized that my poverty and my lack of finance are due to my habits that have been pulling me down. My purse has never been full despite being paid every day for the work I do. Should I continue to blame the gods for my empty wallet or I should blame myself?" Gabriel paused. Larry continued to be puzzled by Gabriel's words.

After the two had been talking for what seemed like an hour, there was a moment of silence. Gabriel noticed that his uncle was no longer responding to what he was saying. "What is it Larry, is everything all right with you?" Gabriel looked at his uncle with a troubled face. Larry coughed and cleared his throat. He looked at Gabriel compassionately. He knew his nephew to be a diligent and honest man. It was for this reason that his siblings were jealous of him. His industry and judicious use of the limited financial resources that came his way had earned him the enmity of his brothers. Unlike his contemporaries, Gabriel didn't indulge in alcohol or smoke cigarettes. Larry had always found Gabriel warm and welcoming, and he would engage with him on critical family problems before making a decision. Consequently, the relationship between the two strengthened after Joshua's death.

"I am here because of you. Would you be interested in working full-time in government at Penrith?" asked Larry. Larry had arranged a job for him to work as a prison officer at Penrith Correctional Services. The chief prison officer at Penrith, James Cook, who had known Larry for many years, had agreed to Larry's request because of his impeccable record in the Department of Road Construction at Penrith. The two had worked for years together before, and at that time Larry was James' supervisor. It was for this reason that Larry was in Roselle. He wanted Gabriel to join Correctional Services the following week. "If I accept this job, Larry, what will it mean for my wife and children?" asked Gabriel. "The choice is yours to make, to or not take it. One option is to move to Penrith with your family if you prefer," replied Larry. Gabriel looked at his uncle and kept quiet for a moment. He knew that he would not be able to commute to and from Penrith in time to start work. He knew too that this would mean leaving his brothers and their families behind. Even if he trusted his uncle, he became scared at the thought of relocating away from his extended family.

These and other thoughts ran through Gabriel's mind. He considered his skills and his limitations for a while, and he remembered that he had no real work experience apart from his labour in the fields in Roselle. He had never written reports, filed documents and any of the tasks which Larry had mentioned earlier. He had never worked in an office, formally employed or worked in prison service. He had seen prison officers securing jails, some carrying weapons, some were in offices, talking on telephones and typing reports. He was overwhelmed by all his limitations and was gripped with fear. He was afraid of prison; he could not imagine himself working for the Correctional Services Department or even wearing their uniform. On the other hand, he was scared of embarrassing his uncle among his peers because of his lack of knowledge. He was afraid of disappointing Larry who had come all the way from Penrith to discuss the offer with him. Gabriel respected Larry but in his head; he could hear voices saying to him "Will you be able to communicate by radio, answer the telephone and be bold enough and know what to say? Will you be able to know how to write reports? Remember, you didn't finish school; you are semi-illiterate. Will you be able to use a typewriter?" Gabriel's older brother Peter had refused a similar job

Steps in the Middle

offer in Penrith a few years earlier because it was far away from home. In those days accepting a position close to one's family was non-negotiable. People would never take jobs more than a cycling distance away. Most people preferred to work within walking distance from home. The offer Larry brought was exactly similar to the offer Peter had rejected years earlier, and so Gabriel wondered what his brothers would say if he were to accept the job offer. He felt that the role was beyond his capabilities. He started thinking of how to reject the offer without disappointing Larry. It was as if a massive load had been placed on his shoulders. Immediately, sweat ran down his spine as he continued to consider the role and his limitations.

After what seemed like a long wait, Larry looked again at Gabriel and he motioned him to wipe sweat pouring down his face. "This must be difficult for you, but I am here to help you," Larry said. "Dad, dad!" Martha interrupted the conversation calling both Gabriel and Larry to come into the house. The two stood up and quietly went inside. Maria had finished cooking, and the table was laid and ready for dinner. The smell of the food whetted their appetites. The kids were in their seats and ready to devour their portion of food. The family and their visitor enjoyed the meal, and later Larry and Gabriel retired to bed without talking about the job offer again.

That night Maria and Gabriel didn't have much sleep. The two reasoned that if Gabriel were to take the job, he would come back and move his family to Penrith. Gabriel had mulled throughout the night over the prospect of leaving his family and taking a job in Correctional Services. He knew he needed a reliable source of income and that; he had to contend with his fears of changing from the work he knew best to the work he had never done. He was aware that Larry wanted to help him and that the job offer would be the solution to his financial woes. He also knew that time was not on his side and if Larry were to leave without him, that would probably be the end of the offer. Gabriel needed to make up his mind and select the best option for him and the family. As for Maria, the possibility of her husband working and earning a stable income would be a big step for the household. Maria also understood the loneliness and misery of a divided family.

When Larry woke up, Gabriel was ready to announce his decision. He knew that he was taking a leap of faith, with the hope that everything will be well with him. Indeed as it is with everyone, life never provides guarantees, and neither was Larry's offer.

Before sunrise, Gabriel woke Larry up to resolve the matter they had discussed the previous day. He knew Larry would have to leave before noon to get to Penrith in time. He told Larry that he had thought long and hard about the job offer, and was willing to go with him and start work. However, his worries of disappointing Larry among his peers, if his performance were to fail to meet the required standard, tormented him. He told his uncle that his handwriting wasn't very legible, that he had never answered the phone in an office, never compiled any records, never worked in a formal job and he had never even earned a salary before. Larry listened patiently while Gabriel listed what seemed like thirty reasons why he was inadequate for the job. He was surprised that Gabriel had come up with so many excuses in just a short while. They all sounded convincing to the extent that he thought Gabriel was asking him to decide for him. On the other hand, Gabriel looked like a child who wanted to jump into a pool but didn't want to get wet. The conversation with Gabriel that morning was in sharp contrast to the courageous and determined man Larry had spoken to the previous day. Gabriel spoke with less assurance when Larry asked him "Where is the strong and confident Gabriel that I talked to yesterday? Was it not you who was talking about changing your life yesterday? You seemed so upbeat about the new ideas of life you had acquired. What has changed overnight?"

"Larry, I want the job, but I am afraid of disappointing you," Gabriel looked imploringly at Larry. "If I don't accept the offer my children will suffer and if I do take the job there is a new hope that life will improve for them."

Larry was certainly confused as to whether Gabriel wanted the job or not and he asked him again, "Are you going with me to take the job or not? Could you make this clear? Look, Gabriel, I am not here to push you into accepting the offer if you are not ready for it. It is perfectly within your right to turn the offer down. I already understand your challenges. I came here with the news knowing fully well that you will have to make your decision. If you decide to go for it, then so be it and if you choose to turn it down, all is well with me. The choice is yours to make." Larry paused and looked at Gabriel and Maria. Larry wondered whether he had not pressurized Gabriel by staying overnight at his house. He wanted Gabriel to make his decision about the job offer, and if Gabriel would not take the job, he had already thought of someone to whom he could extend the offer.

"Larry, I want to take the job offer, and I will be leaving with you this morning," replied Gabriel, looking straight at Larry. He seemed to have mastered his courage and regained his composure. He pulled a cloth from his pocket and wiped his face, and he said "We hope that our lives will be better with the job than without it. I have already discussed this with Maria, and we are both are in agreement regarding this decision." Maria nodded in unison.

"Don't worry," Larry replied, reassuring Gabriel. "You will receive training on the job, and there will be other newcomers when you join. So you will all learn from each other, and soon you will surely master the job. Once you start working, you will build upon your weaknesses, and your fears will start melting away. It is not only men of great character and ability that change the world but also the weak man with determination and ideas," Larry concluded.

Larry's words touched Gabriel's heart, and his countenance began to reflect his renewed confidence. His energy of yesterday began to return to his body. Larry felt happy that Gabriel was going to take the job offer. He knew Gabriel would be a good employee for correctional services and soon James would thank him for his help in getting someone committed and hardworking. Gabriel would be the first among his brothers to hold a formal job in as many generations. Indeed, poverty can be hereditarily passed on from father to son without a break.

Chapter 2

The Family, the relocation and the Penrith Market

Martha and Mark were still asleep when Gabriel finished talking and just when he was ready to leave the house with Larry, they both woke up. "Dad, where are you going? I want to go with you," Mark cried loudly. Gabriel looked at his children, picked them up and comforted them. He walked a few steps toward his wife and looking intently at her, spoke to her in a low tone as if to comfort her too. He talked to Maria for a long time while Larry was standing a few steps away. Maria was standing facing her husband, and Gabriel's shoulders obscured her face. She sounded as though she was sobbing. Gabriel walked backwards as if he was leading Maria back into the house but he stopped at the doorway. He put Martha and Mark down. While he was talking, he placed one of his hands against the wall of the house. He appeared to be persuading his wife to accept the situation and then she quickly walked into the house. Meanwhile, Martha and Mark were still holding firmly to their father's jacket. They both wanted to go along with him as though they had heard their parents' conversation throughout the night. Gabriel had a lot of persuading to do before the two could let him go. Finally, he stepped into the house, and he emerged without his two children, but their crying could still be heard inside the house. Gabriel looked somewhat troubled. This was his first separation from his family, and instead of going drinking with his friends after work, as a non-alcoholic person, he had always been home helping his wife to look after the children soon after returning from the field. As he walked away from his house, he knew it was going to be weeks before he was with his family again. His heart sank at the voices of his children crying behind him, but the crying soon faded away with distance.

Most people in Roselle spent weekends reconnecting with their faith, holding parties and enjoying themselves in local pubs across Roselle. Life in the village was simple and open, and everyone knew a lot about their neighbours. People were accorded respect as befitting their age, and the older women looked out for the children of their community, irrespective of whether they were their own or the neighbours. The community was bound by shared values and common beliefs. People were connected by marriages, language, faith and traditional beliefs.

Martha and Mark finally stopped crying long after Gabriel had left. Maria was still seated on the kitchen stool, leaning against the wall. Her eyes were fixed on her old kitchen cupboard, but her mind was wandering somewhere very far. Her two children had fallen asleep on her lap. She staggered as she stood up to get a glass of water; her dry throat was crying out for water. As she put the kids to bed, she realised they had not eaten anything since morning. She hastened back into the kitchen to prepare food for them. She was still exhausted from lack of sleep the previous night. The couple had slept late after a prolonged evening's discussion regarding their future. It had been a long time since they had engaged in a detailed and thorough conversation of their life together. The decision to take up a full-time job was life-changing, and everything they had was going to be affected.

Maria stared out through the window hoping to see her husband in the distance, but Larry and Gabriel were no longer visible. She looked outside again and noticed that the chickens hadn't been fed, the cows had not been milked and the horses needed to be released into the new paddock. She began to sweat. She was overwhelmed with the tasks requiring her single-handed attention. Gabriel ordinarily looked after the chickens and the livestock, and occasionally Maria would assist when Gabriel was working far from home. They were both hardworking. Maria had recently started rearing chickens for sale. Their numbers had slowly grown in recent months, and now she was ready to start selling them. Gabriel had acquired a small head of livestock and two horses in the last few years from savings. This seemingly insignificant increase in livestock attracted the envy of his brothers.

Peter and Julius, Gabriel's siblings, also relied on casual jobs to provide for their families. They often visited Gabriel's house to borrow tools they needed on their random assignments. Often they came when Gabriel was not at home, and just as often they neglected to return the tools they regularly borrowed. Gabriel would then have to go and fetch his tools from their houses. Julius and Peter would, on occasions, sell Gabriel's tools when they needed money urgently. Maria was reluctant to refuse to give; at the same time, she was equally aware of Gabriel's impatience with his brothers. Occasionally, he would have confrontations with his brothers about his tools, which attracted attention from their wives. Whatever Maria did to please Peter and Julius, had the effect of dividing the extended family and putting her at the centre of controversy. Consequently, Maria became unpopular with their wives, who perceived her as unkind, mean and divisive, notwithstanding that their neighbours knew her to be generous. Gabriel, of course, always stood by his wife despite his anger directed toward his brothers. These family tensions were another cause of the couple's sleepless night before Gabriel left. Maria didn't know how to deal with Peter and Julius without Gabriel's presence at home.

Gabriel was the ninth child in a family of eleven children, eight boys and three girls. As was the custom at the time, all the brothers and their family members lived within walking distance from one another. The family was poor, just like the community in which they lived. Julius and Peter did not progress with education beyond elementary school, as was the case with their wives too. Illiteracy in the family had been passed down from one generation to another; each generation was failing to finish elementary school handed down illiteracy to the next. Peter, Julius and their wives saw no value in education. They neither encouraged it nor opposed it because none of them understood it. Their children also quit school as soon as possible to take up casual jobs within the community. The young minds were lured by the prospect of earning money at an early age. Thus they traded their future for short-term earnings. Instead of attending school, the children worked in fields, trained horses, herded cattle, and sheep, and took up casual jobs in construction and farmers' markets around Roselle.

In some instances, children dropped out of school to help parents provide food for the family, and in others, it was due to sheer lack of direction, encouragement and supervision. Children needed to be taught values and ideals, and that wasn't the case with the wasted youth of Roselle. The parents failed to teach their children how to dream, of a bright and a better future. Perhaps, no one was to blame; one can only explain as good as they know how. Maybe, dreaming can be learnt and self-taught from observation and imagination or, is it?

"Good morning, Maria," Peter bellowed from outside the kitchen window. "Could you please lend me a shovel?"

"Come in Peter," Maria shouted.

"I can't. I need to run to work before it is too late!" came the reply. "I have a big job today. I am digging a storm-water drain at St Paul's Mission, and I am heading there now."

Maria opened the tool room and handed Peter a shovel, the only shovel left after Julius had borrowed another one the previous day. Peter hastened down the road without looking back, and soon he was out of sight. St Paul's Mission was approximately three miles away. Like before, Peter promised to bring the shovel back at the end of the day. Maria remained standing as Peter quickly disappeared. "I hope he'll keep his word," Maria spoke under her breath.

As she locked the tool room, she noticed Peter's two sons, Joshua and Jeff in the distance, walking in the opposite direction to their father. The two were staggering, apparently quite drunk. They were only returning home that morning after being last seen at a nearby pub the previous day. Joshua and Jeff, who had been hired as casual labourers for two days at a nearby plot, had been paid their wages. The pair had then stormed into the pub and had stayed there until the morning when their purses were empty. They were on their way home, struggling to keep their feet steady on the ground and occasionally staggering from one side of the road to the other while shouting to each other at the top of their voices. No one apart from the two could understand what they were saying. In the short time that Maria was locking the tool room, Jeff had fallen several times and each time rising to his feet with a lot of struggle.

Joshua and Jeff were nineteen and twenty-one years old respectively. They had dropped out of Roselle primary school in their early years. They sought pleasure by drinking to excess every time they were paid wages, and they were not the only ones to make headlines in this impoverished community. "My children are not going to be like that; their behaviour is a disaster in waiting." Maria thought. The several times they had been picked up by police had done nothing to change their behaviour; it simply made them known to police more. Indeed, the role of police is not to correct every wrong of society. Could it be that people in Roselle expected too much from the police?

Three weeks after arriving in Penrith with his uncle, Gabriel received training on the job. He soon became friends with several others who were trained at the same time with him, including Ashford Taylor. The two worked in the same section and also cycled from the same residential neighbourhood in Penrith. This strengthened the bond between the two workmates. Correctional Services' officers at Penrith wore uniforms similar to those of the police, and at times people often mistook them for police officers. Correctional Services' officers also carried a weapon at all times during working hours, which they would surrender at the end of every shift. As time went by, some people in Penrith began to recognise Gabriel and Ashford among other Correctional Services officers.

Gabriel had been thinking of bringing his family to Penrith ever since he arrived. After a while, he made Larry aware of his intentions. Larry worked in government for many years and was due to retire in a few years' time, hence was an influential man in Penrith. He was known for his compassion toward people in his community and took pride in servicing their needs. He always showed respect and kindness to both young and old, and this earned him the admiration of his community. He was a fatherly figure to many people, and it was not uncommon for them to come to his house for advice on various aspects of life. As he walked along the streets of Penrith, he would stop to greet people and listen to their stories and crack a joke or two with them before proceeding on his way. He was generous and helped many people who could not afford medical payment or other unforeseen expenses. He had a relatively large area of land where he grazed livestock and cultivated crops. So when Gabriel asked for ideas on where he could settle his family, Larry was quick to introduce him to people who could assist. Within a few weeks, the two walked together into the council offices, and Gabriel was allocated a vacant piece of land in Lockdale, about a mile away from Larry's homestead.

Within a few months, Gabriel arranged for the relocation of his family and all their belongings to Penrith. Gabriel and Maria worked hard to build a new house and an enclosure for their livestock. The regular income Gabriel was receiving significantly improved the family's standard of living. Not only was he able to provide food and clothing, but his savings also grew, and he could afford to spend more time with his children. Maria then returned to her passion, rearing chickens for sale. With family income rising and a beautiful house under construction, the family looked well set for a better life.

About a year after Gabriel's move to Penrith, everything the couple had yearned for previously seemed to be happening. Their income increased further when Maria began to supply chickens and eggs to the Penrith market. Maria and Gabriel made new friends in Penrith where, in those days, it was an honour to be employed by the government to serve people in whatever capacity. Government servants attracted respect and trust from community members. On the other hand, Gabriel's job provided him with more than remuneration. His Correctional Services uniform invited attention from the public, and he became known by name to many people, his relationship with Larry brought him much respect from people in Penrith than he could have imagined.

The primary activity around Penrith was farming. The soils were rich red and black loam. Farmers grew wheat, potatoes, beans and other cash crops for sale at the Penrith market. The people were hard-working, and the farmers' market was a meeting place for the community. Life in this town was quite different to that in Roselle. With good harvests, farmers made decent incomes selling their produce on the market. Competitions were regularly held during the season and prizes awarded to the best entries with winners enjoying the recognition this brought them.

As autumn approached, farmers were busy harvesting summer crops in the fields and as in previous years, looked forward to a bumper harvest. When they brought their produce to the market business was brisk again. There was a high demand for fresh produce with many buyers coming from long distances to place their orders. Fruits and vegetables brought to the market in the early morning would be eagerly purchased before midday, and the farmers would be well rewarded with higher prices. Those who brought produce late would get lower prices, with some barely covering their costs. Most buyers left the market with something they were willing to pay for and so did the farmers. Rarely did someone leave the market empty-handed? The amount depended on the quality of the produce and the time of delivery to the market. Immediately after selling out at the market, farmers would hurry to the shops in town to buy farm implements, chemicals and other supplies before returning to their farms.

Despite the good seasons enjoyed by farmers around Penrith and the business they brought to the market, a dark cloud was looming. The civil war which had been going on around neighbouring towns was slowly creeping closer. To date, no disruption to the farming activity had been witnessed, but things were about to change. The battle between government troops and the rebel army was drawing closer by the day. Penrith was situated on a major trading route linking the east to west of the country. The farms around Penrith were a rich source of food and grain, not only for Penrith but other neighbouring towns as well. The rebel fighters had previously tried to seize the town in an attempt to take control of the food supplies. The government sent more reinforcements and successfully repelled the rebel armies. Although some army checkpoints were erected around the town and the surrounding villages, insurgent attempts on the town became numerous and sustained.

Soon the civil war was at the farmers' doorstep and began to affect farming activities in and around Penrith. Civilian movements became more restricted, and a curfew was put in place. This required business to close shops before sunset and only open the next day after sunrise. Consequently, farmers could no longer bring their produce to the market in the early morning or leave the market after dark as they did in the past. Civilians who disregarded the curfew were often caught in crossfire between government troops and the rebel army. Fatalities and casualties steadily rose. An atmosphere of fear crept in across Penrith and the surrounding towns. With the damage and loss of property, some families, fearing for their lives, started leaving Penrith. The rebels began targeting government infrastructure and systematically disrupting farming activities. Army vehicles carrying troops became a common sight, moving up and down the streets of Penrith and the surrounding villages, day and night. Battles between the opposing armies became a common occurrence around the town. Sometimes battles would commence during the day and often continued into the evening.

One Saturday morning the rebels were seen assembling at Penrith hills. The government troops were soon made aware, and they proceeded to establish their presence closer to Penrith to protect the town from rebel attack. The distance separating the two armies was little less than a mile. The city of Penrith was easily visible from Penrith hills to the south and the Redfern hills, to the north. All the activities and movement of people in town was clearly visible from these hills. In the south, was also a dam, which supplied water to the town and the surrounding farms. The thick bush on the summits of both hills concealed the presence of troops. Penrith market was located less two miles from Penrith hills, and about a mile to the south-east was the Correctional Services building where Gabriel was employed. Directly opposite Correctional Services office were some other government agencies.

The battle continued for several days. Market activities ceased altogether, and residents were confined indoors. The government army, supported by helicopters and heavy machine guns, attacked the rebel stronghold while the rebels fired their guns and mortar shells into the town from Penrith hills, lighting the night sky with a spectacular fireworks display. The exchange of gunfire continued throughout the evening, but when morning came, there was silence as the rebels had retreated.

As the sun rose, a fresh wind blew westwards, and for much of the day the town remained deserted; no one went to the market or came from it. Many people remained indoors still uncertain of security. However, by mid-afternoon people started coming out of their hiding, each one telling stories of what they had heard and experienced. News began to spread of people killed in the crossfire, homes damaged, unexploded ammunition lying in open spaces and the casualties inflicted on both sides. The days that followed were spent in mourning, burying the dead and grieving for the lost ones. A few rebels survived the battle, and the government troops captured some. However, the calm in the town was soon shattered when the rebels attacked again, inflicting casualties on government forces in revenge for the loss of their men. Fighting became more frequent, indiscriminate and more intense. Life in the once prosperous town turned to misery. A few farmers continued bringing produce to the market, but even this trickle of trading soon ceased when some farmers got killed, and part of the marketplace was destroyed. As the news spread, some farmers fled to other towns.

Chapter

3

The army truck and Gabriel's death

For a while, the scene of conflict moved away from Penrith, and apart from a few sporadic incidents, no major battles took place around the town. However, every day the sound of gunfire could still be heard in the distance. One Tuesday afternoon, when the sun's heat was intense, Maria was seated on her patio, absorbed in her thoughts. Gabriel had left for work early that morning as usual. Suddenly a shrill voice broke into her reverie. She looked up and saw a young boy standing outside her gate. "Who are you? What is your name?" she called out as she walked to the gate. Then, she recognised the boy was Thomas, the son of her neighbour. "Has your mother sent you to tell me something?" she continued.

"Mum said you should come to home urgently," replied Thomas. He looked distraught, and his words were barely audible. The boy had already retraced his steps before Maria could reach the gate. Maria hastily shut her door and headed for her neighbour's house. Upon arrival, she saw that many other people were gathered there; men and women from surrounding houses had apparently been summoned and were congregated under a tree in the yard. Everyone was sitting quietly on the ground.

As Maria approached and came in full view of what was going on, she looked in horror when she recognised that the people on the ground were surrounded by eight rebel soldiers, brandishing guns. Their leader was shouting angrily at the top his voice. No one was answering; they were clearly intimidated, their heads hanging down. "What's going on?" Maria asked herself in terror. This was the first time she had come in close contact with the rebel fighters. She had heard about their ruthless conduct in other parts of Penrith. She wanted to run back home, but she realised that if she did so, she could be shot and killed. Her legs wobbled, and her steps became unsteady as she edged closer. "Hey you, get a move on. We are not wasting time waiting for you," shouted the rebel leader. Maria quickened her pace and took a seat amongst the crowd.

The rebel leader was a tall man in his late twenties, clad in a tightly-fitting uniform. He stammered as he spoke and his accent was clearly not known in Penrith. In the many pockets of his uniform were a handgun, a bottle of water and a knife. His hair was in disarray and unkempt as was his beard and his large red eyes swept from one person to another as he spoke. The crowd seated under the tree was mesmerised by his appearance. The eight other men were surrounding the group, also in their mid-twenties, were pointing their guns onto the crowd as if awaiting an order to shoot. The rebels carried a heavy load of ammunition in their backpacks, tightly strapped to their bodies.

As soon as Maria sat down, the rebel leader continued his tirade. "Someone among all of you seated here has passed on information on our whereabouts to the government troops. This resulted in some of our comrades being killed. I have come down here to demand that you show us that person." He looked around at all the people. "We have come here to meet that person who sold information of our movements to government troops," he repeated. His words were greeted with silence. No one spoke, and no one coughed. The look on his face was nerve racking. One could hear the sound of leaves dropping from the Jacaranda tree under which the crowd was seated. The rebel leader asked again for the third time, and still, no one replied; and when he asked for the fourth time, he threatened to shoot and kill everyone unless he was given the information. The captives kept looking to the ground in fear. At last, one old man coughed and cleared his throat as if he was about to speak.

Luke Henderson was a local elder in his late seventies. He had grown up and lived in Penrith all his life, and he knew virtually everyone around the area. He tried to stand up so that he could speak on his feet but his body shook violently, and he fell to the ground. Mr Henderson looked haggard, frail and his face was ashen. His eyes retreated in their sockets and his tongue dried in his mouth. Sweat ran down his grey hair, and his lips became dry and cracked. Mr Henderson rose up again so that he could speak, but again he fell to the ground, and he fainted.

As if he did not care, the rebel leader watched Mr Henderson falling with a thud, turned his back to the prostrate man and repeated his question, this time mouthing the vicious threat with more intensity. The other rebels paid no attention to the stricken old man and focused their attention on their leader. The rebel leader raised his gun and fired randomly into the ground between the people seated. Men, women and children screamed in terror. The bullets hit the ground with such rapidity and ferociousness that clouds of dust filled the air. Mark, Martha, Thomas and other children watching the proceedings from a little distance away, on hearing the sound of gunfire, immediately disappeared from the scene and even the dogs scattered. The rebel leader instructed one of his men to cut a branch from the tree nearby and ordered all men to lay prone on the ground, after that each and every man was beaten mercilessly with the branch. Then they turned to the women where the thrashings were repeated. The rebels continued striking all the people until they were tired. The beatings caused profuse bleeding from the wounds inflicted.

Finally, they picked up their guns and other belongings and took their leave, the leader threatening to return and inflict greater injuries if the information was provided to the government troops again. The rebels hastened down the valley and disappeared to the west of Penrith.

After the ordeal had ended, the victims painfully rose to their feet and walked quietly away from the tree, and headed each to their home. Mr Henderson, who was still lying on the ground, slowly recovered and soon he was able to open his eyes. No one attended to him. He had survived the beating but three other seniors, two male and one female, were severely injured. One of the women was Rose Henderson, Luke's wife. She had suffered a back injury, and she had difficulty rising to her feet. Her blouse had been torn, and she was bleeding copiously from her wounds. Her breathing was hoarse, and she was clearly in deep pain. She clutched her ribs as she tried to speak, but her words were barely audible. Mr Henderson, who had regained consciousness by that time bravely lifted himself up and pulled Rose from the ground and helped her to get home.

There were much sadness and misery in Lockdale, the residential area west of Penrith, the home of many of the people. Those who had suffered the worst injuries from the beatings made their way to Meadow hospital, about a mile south-west of the Penrith market. Maria had been spared severe injuries, but her back was severely bruised, and she was in great pain. She too proceeded to Meadow hospital. The residents from Lockdale, when they arrived at the hospital, were shocked to find that other people from Glebe, Townsend, Dulwich Hill and many other parts of Penrith, had suffered the same fate. It was apparent that the beatings had been inflicted over a wider area by different rebel groups. The rebels' onslaught had been organised at a time when the daily patrols by government troops around Penrith were over. Maria was treated after a long wait, and after being discharged, she headed home with her kids.

Months passed by and the civil war continued unabated. One late afternoon while Martha and Mark were playing close to the house with other children, Larry arrived, expecting to find Gabriel at home. Gabriel had gone to work the previous day and was expected home in the morning but had not yet arrived. It was unusual for Gabriel to come back late or to change shift without telling Maria. But on this day he had not even sent a message home, and Maria was getting anxious.

Larry had not seen Maria since her ordeal at the hands of the rebel troops, a few months earlier. They were talking in the kitchen when suddenly they heard a truck slowing down on the road outside. Maria peered through the window and exclaimed, "It's an army truck!" Larry stood up to look out through the window. The vehicle reduced speed before coming to a complete halt. The lowered his window and spoke to a pedestrian walking along the road who then pointed to Maria's house. The pedestrian looked worried and appeared scared to talk to the driver for a long time. Larry and Maria didn't hear the conversation, but it was clear that the pedestrian was directing the truck driver to Maria' house. Army personnel alighted from the back of the truck to open the gate before the vehicle drove in front of Maria's house.

"This is strange," said Larry. Maria wondered why the government troops were coming to Gabriel's house. She was worried about the beating they had suffered at the hands of rebels a few months earlier. Larry speculated that they were looking for Gabriel. He was worried at the possibility that the soldier was looking for him; he didn't want to be beaten. "Perhaps, I should plead with them to spare me because of my age," he thought. He quickly turned to Maria in panic. "If they point at me, tell them I am a visitor from another state, so they don't beat me."

"Calm down, Larry, calm down!" Maria shouted at Larry as he frantically attempted to find somewhere to hide. Maria and Larry were both sweating and their hearts pounded in unison. She also considered hiding but realised that her children were outside. From the moment she thought about her children outside, she became confused. She looked outside through the window again and noticed that neighbours were also peeping through their windows. Others shut themselves inside and yet others hesitantly came out in the open to have a full view of what was happening, and were prepared to run away should things get ugly.

Army trucks were a threatening sight. When the truck came to a stop at the front door, neither Larry nor Maria ventured out. Then one of the soldiers shouted out Maria's name. She went out running, confused and shaking uncontrollably. She wasn't sure how they knew her name or whether she had been accused of doing something wrong. "Are you the wife of Gabriel?" the soldier asked. Larry, who was standing at the door; not wanting to be seen, eventually came out from hiding and followed Maria outside; hesitant and unsure of what would happen to him. He joined Maria who was talking with one of the soldiers. The truck driver and the rest of the soldiers at the back of the truck stayed in the vehicle but listened attentively to the conversation. The soldier began addressing Maria and Larry. His voice was grim.

"I am very sorry to tell you that your husband was killed by rebels this morning on his way home. We have brought his body with us. It is on the back of the truck." He said pointing at the truck.

"What do you mean?" Larry asked the soldier, but he declined to answer or clarify further. Instead, he beckoned the soldiers on the back of the truck to take down the body. They gently lifted Gabriel's body from the truck and quietly carried it into the house on a canvas stretcher. They lifted the body from the stretcher bed and laid it on the floor and wrapped it in a white cloth.

"Can you verify this is Gabriel's body?" asked the soldier after bending down to uncover Gabriel's face. Larry nodded in agreement. It was apparent that Gabriel had died from bullet wounds and after that, no one dared to look at his body for the second time. Maria found it heart-wrenching to watch what was left of Gabriel's body.

The soldier ordered that Gabriel is buried as soon as possible and gave strict instructions regarding weeping and that no one should make any noise. The soldier marched out of the house. "Get me a bucket full of water," one of the soldiers demanded. He took the bucket to the back of the truck and sluiced the blood out.

The soldiers jumped back onto the truck, and the truck departed down the road without any further explanation.

Maria fell to her knees in pain and shock. Energy drained out of her body. Her world seemed to have come to an abrupt end. She dragged herself into the dining room where the soldiers had left Gabriel's body in the white-blooded cloth. She cried out with deep emotion and grief. Tears ran down her cheeks, and she was overcome with confusion. She spoke to her husband's corpse as if she expected an answer.

The neighbours watched the army truck with anxiety and were ready to run away, suddenly got relieved when the truck departed. Others were worried that the rebels would come back upon hearing that the community had a visit from government troops. Suddenly everything changed when they heard that Gabriel had been killed that morning and that his body had been brought by the army truck. Then they heard Maria crying uncontrollably, some at first thought the soldiers had beaten her. When they entered Maria's house, she was still sobbing, sitting next to Gabriel's bullet-riddled body. The blood from his wounds had soaked the white sheet which wrapped his body. His blood marked a trail from where the truck had stopped at the house. The neighbours helped Maria to make burial arrangement and immediately Larry sent messages to Gabriel brothers to be present at the funeral, scheduled for the next day. He arranged for a carpenter to make a wooden coffin from the timber that Gabriel had left over after completing the construction of his house.

Mark and Martha were outside, playing with their friends, oblivious to the tragedy that had befallen them. They had no real understanding of why people were gathered at their house. One woman called Mark and asked him, "Do you know your father has been killed? You must come into the house and see his body?" Mark looked at the older woman, feeling shy and unsure what was expected of him. He smiled, and it was apparent that the concept of death wasn't clear to neither him nor Martha, who was standing next to him. They were still too young to understand and hence their reaction was rather confused. They only learned that something had happened to their father. In their young minds, they probably thought death was temporary, and therefore Gabriel would wake up later. Mark saw his father body being offloaded from the truck, taken into the house and the blood being cleaned from the truck, and after that, he went back to play with others.

Maria was pregnant with her third child and would be giving birth in three months' time. Rose Henderson was worried that Maria's health would deteriorate and she would lose her child. She did her best to comfort Maria and together with other older women tried to console and support Maria given her physical condition. They looked after Maria throughout her period of mourning, anxiety and the depression that followed.

By the end of the day, the news of Gabriel's death had reached his brothers and Maria's parents, all of whom arrived in Penrith in time for the burial. For a while, Lockdale became enveloped in a sombre mood. The death of Gabriel was the first and closest to home that the civil war had claimed in Lockdale. Maria and Gabriel were due to celebrate six years of marriage in a few months, and by all measures, the couple appeared to have been doing well. Both were hard-working individuals. People mourned the fact that the death of Gabriel had robbed the family of a promising and industrious father. Gabriel was a real example of an ambitious individual whose life and future had been cut short by a rebel bullet. The following day, people from all over Penrith who knew Gabriel from his work with the Correctional Services Department attended his burial at Lockdale Cemetery which was a short distance from his house.

That fateful morning Ashford and Gabriel had cycled together from work when shots were fired from a distance. Gabriel sustained multiple shots to his head and chest and died on the spot. Ashford, who was lightly wounded by bullets, was picked up and taken to a hospital. He was still recovering from the shooting incident and was unable to attend the funeral.

Martha and Mark still found it difficult to comprehend where their father had gone, although their mother and others tried to explain his demise. The idea of death never took hold in their hearts. The absence of their father was never fully resolved, and for the following year, the two continued to talk about their father and played games in which one of them pretending to be him. Such role-playing affected Maria deeply and made her life difficult to bear.

Chapter 4

The promise that never was

In the days and weeks that followed Gabriel's death, life became difficult for Maria. Although some friends sympathised with her loss, regularly coming to her house to console her and give her company, others paid no attention to her situation. Her title soon changed in keeping with her husband's death and everyone started addressing her in the way they found it fit. Some addressed her as the wife of the deceased; some called her the widow and yet others described her as the mother of the orphaned children. She felt that the respect she had when Gabriel was alive was slowly eroding. She became lonely and missed the companionship of friends, who used to frequent her when her life was going well. The challenges of looking after children alone were beginning to weigh her down. She missed the experience and joy of watching her kids play with their father. With no choice left, she had to assume the role of both father and mother.

Steps in the Middle

Maria was only twenty-six years old when Gabriel was tragically killed. Her marriage had come to an abrupt end. Her parents lived far away, and she was still a relative new-comer in Penrith where they had relocated. In her induction to married life, nothing had prepared her for the sudden death of Gabriel and how to move on with life after his death. She had hoped the two would reach old age together. The marriage had ended at a time that prosperity seemed to be on its way. Their dream of becoming successful looked set to be within grasp. Maria was still learning to be a better wife and mother to her children. She had not yet experienced much of what married life is about.

Within a short time of grieving her loss, Maria found herself being forced to rise and respond to the challenges of single parenthood; which required her to be the sole provider and head of the family. She knew very well that the society of the day didn't treat kindly single mothers. There were societal prejudices she had to become accustomed to. There weren't many single parents in Lockdale. "If you are a single parent, no one looks after you and often people forget that single parents exist. People forget that single parents also have needs," Maria said to herself. She realised that as a young woman, her parents had focused on teaching her how to be a good mother and how to raise a family, but had never prepared her for the possibility of losing a mate.

Maria felt in need of counselling, and all she got were random voluntary counselling sessions from older women who had come to know her in the short time her family had relocated to Penrith. Some older women counselled her against talking to married men as if her priority was to look for another man. She recalled an instance when Julius asked to speak to her, and Julius' wife rudely demanded to be present. It was as if she was making a clear statement to her to stay away from Julius, even if Maria had not asked for the meeting.

She had not been attending church meetings for some weeks after Gabriel's death. Then she and her children eventually started attending congregation meetings at Dulwich, another residential area in Penrith near their home in Lockdale. One Sunday afternoon a woman, apparently forgetting that Gabriel had died, asked her, "Where is your husband these days; we don't see you together?"

Even though the question was sincere, Maria was overcome with sadness. She answered, "My husband passed away a few months ago."

"Oh, I am sorry to hear that. What happened and how are you coping with the kids alone?" Maria explained everything that had happened to her husband, and then walked away, holding her children by the hand. Her pregnancy was nearly getting to a full team, and everyone was awed by her seeming bravery, and yet deep inside she was battling to hold. Then another person noticed the absence of her husband and asked her the same questions, and she repeated the same answer. She felt as if she was revealing her misfortune to the congregation in return for an expression of sympathy. She was embarrassed by constantly talking about her loss to everyone in the congregation and exposing her vulnerability. The feeling of shame gripped her; people looked at her as if she had lost a valuable jewel through her fault. She was uncomfortable at being constantly reminded of the death of her husband and having to recount what had happened. The one question she hated most was, "Oh sorry, so what are you going to do with the kids now?"

"I am not going to church again for the next few months," she said to herself in despair. "I'm tired of being asked the same questions." She acknowledged that the church was a source of spiritual comfort, but the members of the church were ordinary people who got curious and asked her questions that were too personal and caused her discomfort. Indeed, this was a reflection of the society in which Maria lived at the time. As days passed, time soon proved to be the greatest healer of broken hearts.

One day, Maria was preparing to go to the market with her children, and as they walked out of the kitchen door, a man was standing outside. Mark and Martha ran to the gate shouting, "Dad, dad, dad!" They had mistaken him for their father, and when they reached him, he picked the two children up together, just as their dad used to do. Maria's stood motionless at the doorway. Her heart sunk when she heard the children greeting the man at the gate and she was overcome by emotion. Her legs felt weak, and she had to find somewhere to sit before she fell. Tears ran down her cheeks. It turned out that the man was delivering a letter from Correctional Services Department where Gabriel was previously employed. The man's uniforms resembled the Gabriel used to wear on duty. The man put the kids down, and he said, "I have come to deliver this letter from Correctional Services. Could you please sign this book for madam to evidence that you have received the letter?"

Maria's hands struggled to hold the pen firmly as she scribbled her signature before the man left. She opened the letter to read, but the events of the past few minutes had affected her to the extent that she couldn't focus her mind. She staggered back into the house, collapsed on the couch and in a short time fell fast asleep. Meanwhile, Martha and Mark continued to play outside the house oblivious to their mother's struggles. For many days that followed, Maria's appetite disappeared. She would not eat or drink properly.

The next day Maria and her children left for the Correctional Services office, in windy and chilly weather. She was required to sign papers and provide details of her bank account so that she could receive a pension. At one point Maria considered leaving Martha and Mark in the care of Matilda, Larry's wife, but the distance to Larry's house was too daunting for her. Matilda was a mature woman whose health had deteriorated with advancing age and lifestyle choices. Maria remembered Matilda's joy when she and the children first arrived in Roselle, and the support Matilda had given her in settling down in Penrith.

"Those were the good times," she thought. She remembered Matilda's cooking and the moments they had shared together at Matilda's house. It had been a beautiful Saturday with a clear blue sky when Matilda invited Maria and Gabriel for lunch. Maria had woken up early to prepare the kids for a visit. When they were both dressed in their best weekend outfits, Gabriel and Maria had left their house, each holding a child by the hand. When they arrived at Larry's house, a delicious smell of roasted beef welcomed them from the backyard. They entered the house, but Gabriel could not sit for long before disappearing to join Larry in the garden. Matilda was preparing fish, rice, roast potatoes, vegetables, gravy, scones and a variety of salads with fruit and ice-creams to end with.

"I am ready!" Matilda shouted as she brought the food out in the warmth of midday sunshine. The weather had been generous that day and was a sharp contrast to the rainy and chilly days that characterised the previous weeks. Larry brought the meat he had prepared. It was roast beef, pork and chicken; and in no time the table was full. The two families sank in their chairs around the elongated table in the shade. "It was such a festive and exciting day," Maria thought as her mouth began to water with the memories of the occasion.

Matilda and Larry had never been blessed with a child and their inability to conceive drove Matilda into depression. She found solace in drinking beer to excess with friends. Although Maria had a cordial relationship with Matilda, on the many occasions that she visited Matilda, she would find her drunk. Matilda wouldn't accept that she had become an alcoholic and she vehemently refused to get help. She couldn't let a day pass without opening a bottle of beer, and indeed every time she indulged herself, her worries seemed to disappear. One day Maria left her children in the custody of Matilda when both Larry and Gabriel had both gone to work. When she returned to collect her children, she found Matilda too drunk to speak or walk. The kids had not been fed, and their lunch boxes were still in their bags. Before leaving with her hungry children, she helped Matilda onto her bed and closed the door behind her. Since that day, she never left her children with Matilda, nor did she speak about the incident to Gabriel or Larry. In time, Matilda's drinking problems worsened, and she relied on alcohol to avoid facing life's worries.

A year had gone by since Gabriel's death when a memorial was organised for him. Peter and Julius and their wives travelled from Roselle to attend the event. Maria's brothers Benedict, Conrad, Patrick and Sylvester Taylor, who had travelled all the way from Casterbridge, a distance of about a hundred and twenty miles away, were also present at the memorial. It had been a year since they had last seen Maria and her children. Maria's elder sister, Prisca together with Agnes, Maria's mother, arrived a day before the event.

Maria had given birth to a baby girl, her third child whom she named Masculine, in memorial of her husband's loss. When the memorial celebration was held Masculine was nearly nine months old, and a very active child she proved to be. The pressure of single parenthood was taking a toll on Maria, who had three mouths to feed. The increase in the size of her family also came along with greater attention needed by the children. Single-handedly, she struggled to care for their emotional needs.

After everyone had taken lunch, Larry summoned Maria's parents to a meeting to discuss the children's welfare and custody of her property. He addressed them with these words: "We must put our heads together and make a collective decision along with Maria regarding the future of her children and their property. I am concerned about their welfare as life has been difficult for them since Gabriel's death. Maria and the children are not managing. As for me, I am old, and I can't help then very much. Maria will need someone mature to console and support her. I am asking you to consider taking Maria back with you so that you can help her and the children."

Larry paused and looked at Maria's parents. There was silence for some moments. Then Sylvester, Maria's eldest brother, cleared his throat and said, "I was shattered by the tragedy that struck my sister's family, and I have heard your point, Larry. Gabriel was taken unexpectedly to the great darkness," He looked at Maria. "What is your position regarding Larry's proposal?" Suddenly all eyes were on her.

Maria gathered her thoughts for a few minutes before she began to speak. She had not yet come to terms with Gabriel's death. The loss was still a fresh wound in her heart. Sylvester's question had brought into focus the downward spiral her life had taken since her loss. She had developed wrinkles which ran from

Steps in the Middle

one side of her face to the other. Her cracked palm bore witness to her untold struggles with life since Gabriel died. Tears ran down her cheeks not because of the question Sylvester had asked her but the perceived difficulties lying ahead of her. She raised her head and glanced at Martha and Mark who were seated quietly in the room, and fresh tears spurted from her eyes.

After a long pause, Maria responded, "It is true that I am not coping alone. I think it is better if I go back to stay with Mum. I need help looking after the livestock and doing the house chores. My parents can certainly help with the kids when I go to the market."

After a lengthy conversation, Sylvester turned to Larry and said, "I am happy that you had given this matter some thought before we came here and that you had explored the best way forward for the family. Maria is free to return to Casterbridge, along with her children." Agnes and Prisca, who were listening attentively, nodded in agreement. Sylvester continued, "But you must know this, Larry, Maria's children remain a joint responsibility between your family and my family. The death of Gabriel should not end your interaction with his children, and neither should your request mean a transfer of responsibility to Casterbridge. Gabriel's children remain your responsibility too, even if we will accommodate them in Casterbridge."

Sylvester paused and looked at his brothers as if to invite them to comment further. But Benedict, Conrad and Patrick only nodded in agreement and so did Julius, Peter and their wives. Everyone appeared to be still in shock of Gabriel's death even if a year had just passed. Sylvester spoke eloquently as his explanation resonated with the customs of people at the time. These were people who shared a common culture and whose beliefs were deeply entrenched. They believed in a patrilineal society in which children were considered to belong primarily to the male parent and adopted their father's name. Upon marriage, women immediately assumed the husband's surname and became part of a new family.

Larry spoke next. "Regarding Gabriel's assets and livestock, Maria and I discussed this with Julius and Peter, and we agreed that they should take over custody of all the things Gabriel possessed. They should look after the livestock, allow them to multiply and keep them for Gabriel's children until such time they are grown up."

He explained the custody arrangement. "If and when any of the children are in need of significant financial help, they will go and discuss the details with Peter and Julius, who will arrange for some of the possessions to be sold to provide money as might be required." Larry made it clear that Peter and Julius would hold the possessions of the late Gabriel in trust and not for their needs. Peter and Julius, in turn, confirmed Larry's words and expressed their willingness to care for the future needs of their late brother's wife and children. Larry also requested Julius and Peter to visit Gabriel's children after their relocation to Casterbridge regularly. The meeting concluded with Larry thanking Sylvester, Conrad, Patrick and Benedict for their understanding and willingness to look after Maria and her children

Chapter 5

The trip back to her childhood home

After Gabriel's memorial, Maria began preparing to relocate with her children to Casterbridge. She knew it would be years before she would be in Penrith again. Maria loved her home. She had developed an emotional attachment to her house, and it was one of the happy reminders of her marriage with Gabriel. Their dogs, Snoopy and Paw, were fond of their home, both having their comfortable place to retire for the night. It was difficult to leave all the possessions they had acquired and made a fresh start in Casterbridge, although it was her childhood home nearly ten years earlier.

"This is the only place my children can really call home," she thought. Martha and Mark had separate bedrooms, and her house had plenty of space for the kids to feel comfortable. "I wish I could carry all this and take it with me," Maria said to herself as she looked at the new king-sized bed she bought a few months before Gabriel's death.

"How much will the pawn shop pay me for the dining table and chairs, the lounge suite and the rest of my furniture? If transport costs were not so high, I would have moved all the furniture along with the remainder of the family's belongings, to Casterbridge," She kept pondering.

But then she realised that she was moving in with her mother, who already had a lot of furniture. Her mother's house had an extra bedroom which she was going to occupy. She knew Agnes was generous given her bereavement. "If I had a choice, I wouldn't go back to Casterbridge. I would stay in my house with my children. But I don't have that choice. I am feeling lonely in this house, and I can't manage with the kids." Tears streamed down her face at these thoughts.

Just then she looked outside as the truck from the pawn shop arrived. All the goods she had put aside for sale were loaded, and the truck departed down the street without delay. She had been paid a paltry sum for the furniture. The money she had received was still in her hands. "I think they have got all the furniture at a bargain," she thought. "I can't replace my furniture with this amount of money; it is well below the market price of my stuff," Maria thought as she looked at the money. "It feels like I have been robbed. This is not fair. Why do pawn shops exist, is it not to reap people and if that is true, they have just stolen from me with my eyes open."

Feeling sorry for herself for yet another loss, she went inside the house, and she began feeling like she was in a strange place. There was nowhere to seat, her couch, the dining room table and chairs had gone. Every sound she made it echoed throughout the house and Maria was upset. Everything that had provided comfort and a sense of home were no longer hers, she had seen her furniture being taken away from here, and somehow she doubted whether that was the right decision to make. One thought kept telling her to stay in her house and work her way with time. The thought kept comforting her that everything would be already with time. For a moment, her thoughts almost convinced her to go after the truck from the pawn shop and bring back her furniture. Staying put in her house sounded a wise thing.

Another thought kept telling her that she wouldn't cope with the children alone. Whatever the best decision to make was, Maria decision to move seemed to be driven more by loneliness and fear of the future. She wasn't ready and healthy emotionally to stand and face her fears alone. Her emotions were still fragile and delicate. She yearned for her mother to comfort her and someone to stand by her like Gabriel did. She was not yet ready to transition into single parenthood, and even if she were willing, she didn't know where to start.

Martha and Mark were enjoying themselves in the house, running through the empty rooms without needing to dodge any furniture as before. She looked at them as they ran after each other, laughing ecstatically. Maria's face softened, and she smiled, when her thoughts were interrupted by her children in the house. Her kids had become her only source of comfort and a precious symbol of her marriage to Gabriel. Although in the first few months after Gabriel's death Martha and Mark were bewildered by the absence of their father, with time they stopped asking about his whereabouts. They learnt to enjoy playing with each other, and Maria was surprised at the level of happiness her children seemed to enjoy while she was experiencing such misery.

Two days after the furniture had been removed, Maria went down to Glebe to bid farewell to Larry and Matilda and to her dogs, Snoopy and Paw, that Larry had collected a week after the memorial. They discussed the future of Maria's house. Larry suggested that the house should be rented until the children had grown up in case they would be interested in returning to their parents' house. He offered to find tenants for the house and administer the property on Maria's behalf, and Maria agreed with Larry's proposal. Before she left Matilda's house, they gathered once more under the shade of the tree as they had done more than two years earlier, only now Gabriel was no longer present, and Maria had three children. They knew it would be a long time before they would meet each other again.

Maria also had to face the fact that she was going to leave Mark behind in the care of Matilda and Larry. She knew Matilda had her struggles with alcohol and giving her custody of her son wasn't the best idea. Were it not for Larry who had asked for Mark to remain behind with him; she wouldn't have agreed to leave him behind. Maria had deep respect for Larry, and it was for this reason that she had agreed to his request. Larry was a very responsible man, who could put up with the challenging situation for long and took personal responsibility when necessary. As she walked away from their home, Maria hoped everything would be alright with Mark, although the parting with Mark was sad for both of them. However, she was resolute that soon she would be back to fetch Mark. Her fervent wish was that Matilda would exercise restraint with her drinking until she was back to fetch Mark.

After lunch, Maria left with Martha and Masculine and returned home leaving Mark behind. It was an emotional parting as Mark suddenly wanted to go with his mother. After a lot of persuasions, Mark agreed to remain behind and that subsequently made parting easier for Maria. On her way home, Maria she went past her friends' houses, bidding farewell to them. When she finally got to Rose Henderson's place, the two women embraced each other intensely and wept together as if they would never see each other again. Rose had become a mentor to Maria since Gabriel's death. She had taken it upon herself to provide emotional support to her friend but the injuries inflicted by the assault on her body more than two years earlier meant she couldn't walk to Maria's house as often as she wanted to.

The following day Maria woke up early and fed Martha and Masculine. The day of their departure to Casterbridge had arrived, and in a short while the vehicle taking them drove in and parked outside ready to load her belongings. The driver loaded all her belongings which filled the van to capacity. They boarded the vehicle, and as they sped down the road, Maria realised that her time in Penrith was over. She was leaving with mixed feelings. It was so sad to go without Gabriel and Mark, and yet the memories of her life in Penrith had also been happy ones.

As they drove away from Lockdale and eventually out of Penrith, Maria knew life would not be the same again. "Everything in life comes to an end, but I didn't think this would be the end of my life in Penrith. It was indeed so brief, just like morning mist that appears and in no time quickly vanishes, so was my life in Penrith. There was no warning and no signs. I can't change anything now; it is now water under the bridge anyway. I am going to do whatever it takes to look after my children. They are not going to lack anything," she thought. She clenched her fists and patted it against her lap, absorbed in her thoughts, her lips quivering, and her eyes fixed on the dashboard of the van as if she was concerned with the speed they were travelling.

Maria wondered whether there was any way Gabriel's death

could have been avoided. She pondered over many questions which she was not able to answer. Was it sheer misfortune or some punishment from the creator for something she had done? What would have happened if Gabriel had not taken the job at Correctional Services? Perhaps he would be alive, and the family would still be together. If Gabriel had continued working on casual jobs, would they still be living happily together and would the kids have grown up with a father? She questioned whether she had been the moving force in Gabriel's decision to relocate to Penrith. Was she responsible for Gabriel's death because she had encouraged him to take up the job? If she had refused to move, surely he wouldn't have taken up the job in Penrith. She remembered that Gabriel was initially very fearful of going to Penrith.

"Oh, it's my fault!" Maria panicked at the thought, and she sobbed. The driver, who had been watching Maria closely since they had started the journey, brought the van to a stop. "Madam, what's wrong? Can I help you with something?" He took some tissues from the dashboard and handed them to Maria whose face was wet with tears, her eyes swollen. Some of her tears landed on Masculine who was fast asleep on her lap.

"Whatever it is, hold on a few more minutes. We will reach our destination shortly," the driver said and started the engine. Maria wiped the tears from her face, but she remained silent as the vehicle started moving. In the rear seat, Martha felt sad as she watched her mother wipe tears from her eyes. She knew there was something wrong, but she was unsure what to do to help. Suddenly she became confused and worried. She was nearly crying when the driver offered her some sweets. She stretched her hand to receive the sweets, but she didn't put any of the sweets in her mouth. It was like she didn't have an appetite for sweets, although she couldn't resist stretching her hand to get hold of them.

At last, they arrived in Casterbridge. Maria and the children entered the house, and all her property was crammed into the one room which Agnes had allocated to her. Agnes was experienced in handling children. She was looking after Dominic and Thandi, the children of her eldest daughter, Prisca, who seventeen years earlier divorced her husband. After the divorce, Prisca went on to take a job in another town a short distance west of Casterbridge, where she was employed as a domestic helper for nearly ten years. As was common with domestic servants at the time, Prisca lived with her employer and didn't come home regularly. She could spend up to six months before returning to Casterbridge. Whenever she could, she sent money home to support her children, although some months passed without Agnes hearing from her.

Agnes also looked after two other grandchildren, Bernard and Elizabeth, Benedict's children from his first marriage. Benedict was in another relationship, and he was still negotiating with his new wife about taking over the custody of the children.

When Maria arrived with Martha and Masculine, the total number of grandchildren in Agnes's house increased to six. Agnes now had grandsons and granddaughters of all age groups. Dominic and Thandi were twins and were fourteen years old at the time. Bernard and Elizabeth were eleven and eight years old. Martha was five and Masculine was two. Despite the different ages of her grandchildren, Agnes was gentle and lovingly cared for them all. She taught them discipline, respect and assigned chores as an essential part of their training. The children learnt how to handle every task in a rotation. Agnes was a patient teacher and fairness was her hallmark. She enjoyed playing with the children and rarely lost her temper. She seemingly had endless time for them. Every morning she woke up to assign each child a task to do, indoors or outdoors, and once they completed their duties, Agnes would come and inspect their work. If the work is done to her satisfactions, the assigned person would be rewarded with a warm hug and the children liked her way of acknowledging their effort.

The children soon learnt that doing their chores properly made Agnes happy the whole day. When they did wrong, she would not be happy, and she would not smile at them that day. As an experienced granny, she would tell stories every weekend or during school vacations when the children were home. She would gather them in her living room after dinner and say good bedtime stories until they all fell asleep.

A few months after Maria settled in Casterbridge, she sought business opportunities in the town. She decided that the buying of farm produce from suppliers in bulk and selling to various markets offered viable opportunities for her. Selling was something with which she was already experienced although the profit margins were low and the cost of transport of fruit and vegetables was high. Selling farm produce was a risky business because stock easily got spoilt. But this was a challenge she had to master. To make matters worse, Casterbridge unlike Penrith, had few commercial farms that supplied fresh produce and therefore she had a limited source of supply. At that time, selling farm produce was a male-dominant sector, and she faced discrimination in a community where many women weren't in gainful employment.

However, in time Maria's business grew, and she started supplying fresh farm produce to households, supermarkets and other markets. Then she stopped selling fruit and vegetables and started supplying fish, meat and chicken. She became an agent for fuels such as diesel and paraffin, as well as for clothes, school uniforms and textbooks. She did anything she could to earn money and was profitable. She hoped that her children would go to school and grow up to achieve the wealth and enjoy comforts she and Gabriel had always hoped for. She felt it was her duty to regain all they had lost in Penrith.

One day Maria was walking back home after a long and busy day at the market. She had sold out early that day and didn't need to hire transport to bring any unsold stock home. She was tired and the day was hotter than usual. It was not just the heat from the scorching sun that was making her uncomfortable, but the hunger pangs from her empty stomach. Maria's pace slackened as she walked through the last residential streets before getting home.

"Let me take a rest for a few minutes in the park, and I will be on my way soon," she thought. She found a spot in the shade which gave her respite from the burning heat. Maria wiped her face seeming unconcerned with the children playing in the park. As she sat with her back against the tree trunk, suddenly she fell asleep. She began to dream walking with Mark into an orchard. All the trees in the orchard had fruits ripe and ready for picking, but she was short to pick any fruit. There was no ladder to climb so that she could pick the fruits. She decided to lift Mark on her shoulders so that he could stand and reach the branches of the tree. When Mark stood on her shoulders, he was able to pick as many fruits and possible, after which they sat down, ate and were filled. They both filled their bags with as many fruits as they were able to carry and they went their way.

She must have been lost to the dream world for nearly an hour when unbeknown to her the weather began to change. Thick dark clouds replaced the blue sky. The wind changed direction and started blowing westwards. The birds took shelter as branches were whipped violently from side to side. The sky became dark and people, young and old, hurried out of the park. Maria was woken when the hailstones started coming down accompanied by cold rain and strong wind. It was not possible for Maria to take refuge elsewhere and therefore she remained under the tree, sheltering from the weather.

It was dark when the rain stopped, and Maria walked home. Soaked from head to toe, she arrived home shivering. Her clothes were dripping water. Martha and Masculine leapt from their granny's arms upon hearing their mother's voice. They ran towards Maria, and she leant forward and lifted them up with both her hands. "Go and put on warm, dry clothes first," Agnes shouted as Maria walked into the house. Martha and Masculine were not bothered by their mother's wet clothes; her presence brightened their mood.

"Mum! Granny taught me how to count today, and I can count now," Martha declared excitedly as she started counting. The kids were always happy to see their mother back. They had become accustomed to welcoming her home at that time of the day. Maria longed for a day she could spend at home without having to worry about earning money. But that was the cost of single parenthood. She needed to save money for the kids' education, and soon Mark would be old enough to go to school.

It had been more than a year since she had left Mark in the care of Matilda and Larry in Penrith. On several occasions, she had written to Larry enquiring about Mark, and she had promised more than once to come and fetch him. Each time she set a date to travel, something would come up, and she would not be able to make the trip. Money was one of the primary reasons for postponing the trip to Penrith. The pension she was receiving from Correctional Services and the rent receipts she was receiving from her house in Penrith was barely enough to take care of the children's expenses.

The income from her business was unpredictable. She had to be bailed out by Agnes on a couple of occasions when she made losses due to unsaleable stock. She had also lost money on various business ventures, twice she had been robbed, more than once she lost money in unsaleable stock and many times she thought of quitting, but she kept her hopes alive out of necessity. She was desperate to provide for her children, and the financial losses made the situation even more punishing. Although the profit-making purpose of establishing business was clear to her, selling agricultural commodities was a volatile and challenging business. One day she would sell her produce before midday and make a good profit, and on another day she would only run out late in the day and barely breaking even, and in yet other instances she would make a loss.

"What else can I do to make a profit?" she mused. "I work every day of the week and have no day of rest. If I stop this business, I will not be able to raise money for my kids to go to school. I'll just have to keep trying until I succeed."

Maria stopped outside a bookstore. "My son will be going to grade one next year, and I want to buy books for him," she thought. The headmaster of Casterbridge Primary School had told her that all Grade One books were available at the store now in front of her. Maria entered and approached the saleslady.

"Do you know what books I need for Grade One?" she asked

"Yes madam, it is mid-year now, and most schools have already bought books, but still we have sufficient stock", replied the saleslady pulling a file from under her desk. "Do you want the full set or the half set?" she asked.

"What is the difference?" Maria asked.

"The full set has all the colouring books and coloured pencils needed by children until they finish Grade One. The half pack is cheaper, but if you buy it, you will need to come back again during mid-year and purchase the remainder."

She explained the price difference, and it was clear to Maria that the full set was cheaper, so she paid for it and left. She entered another shop down the street to buy school uniform. She was determined to provide for the future that Gabriel wanted the kids to have. He had often talked about the importance of education and the misery they would endure without proper education. This made such an impression on Maria's heart that she resolved to do everything within her power to ensure that the children didn't miss out on education. She knew how much Gabriel regretted dropping out of school. As uneducated adults, they did not have access to well-paid jobs. This had become the driving force for Maria to work every day for the better life which Gabriel had dreamt of providing. She was determined to fulfil the wishes of Gabriel. Perhaps he would be happy to know that she was carrying out his vision. She headed home, carrying in one hand a bag of books and in another the school uniforms for Mark, who was yet in Casterbridge.

A few months after Maria's school purchases, the civil war ended. Life in the towns and villages slowly returned to normal, and people began to move freely from one location to another. It was at this time that Larry wrote again to Maria describing how Matilda's health had deteriorated. She had been in and out of the hospital, and that he had just returned home from the hospital with Matilda that week. "Mark is doing well and has grown up a lot since you left. In fact, he has been a valuable companion for Matilda when I am at work," wrote Larry. "With the civil war just ended, I think Mark will be ready to go to school next year. I will find him a school close to our house if you are not ready to come and fetch him."

Although Larry did not ask Maria directly to fetch Mark, it was clear that the time was ripe for her to do so. Maria looked at her nearly empty purse and resolved that the next time she made a profit she would go immediately and fetch Mark from Penrith.

Chapter 6

When all that was left is lost

Agnes was born and raised in a family of devout Catholics. Both her mother and father came from a long line of Catholics. Not surprisingly, she too married a Catholic. Agnes's husband died in the prime of their married life due to alleged poisoning that occurred during a family party. Agnes had only one sister, Aletta, and five brothers. Keith was Agnes's last born brother. Being the eldest in her family, Agnes commanded respect from her siblings. Following in the family tradition, Aletta became a Catholic nun a few years after junior school and Keith became a priest later after completing high school. Aletta resided at the Catholic convent at St Columbus mission which runs a primary school and a high school, as well as an orphanage.

For years, Aletta worked alongside various priests visiting nearby parishes. She became well-known and respected in the community. The mission was located on the outskirts of the town of Hartley, a city known for its beautiful residences and affluence compared to many towns around it. It was a town renowned for its gold and nickel mines which employed Agnes's brothers and their sons. Keith practised his priestly duties at Marist Mission, some several hundred miles west of Hartley. Because of the remote location and his priestly duties, he rarely came to visit Agnes. On the other hand, Aletta frequented her sister's home, bringing gifts from the various parishes she visited.

On one occasion, when Aletta visited Agnes with her many gifts, she stayed overnight which was not her usual practice. During a special lunch that Agnes had prepared for her, they opened their hearts to each other as they often did in the past and discussed many topics.

"How is Maria and how is she managing?" asked Aletta. Agnes looked at her sister and continued to stir her cup of coffee without answering the question. Aletta was puzzled since Agnes always responded to her questions immediately. She suspected something was worrying her and she didn't persist with her question. At that time of the day, Maria was not yet home as she would only be back from the market in the evening. The six grandchildren took their positions around the table and quietly began partaking their lunch. In no time everyone was done, and the children set about their tasks as they had been taught; one cleared the table, another washed the dishes, and yet another cleaned the house and so on. Soon they were playing outside again.

Aletta turned to her sister. "Now tell me, Agnes, is there anything troubling you?" She looked into Agnes's tearful eyes. Agnes shook her head and motioned her to follow her outside the house. The two walked outside the house to take advantage of the cool breeze of the late afternoon.

Agnes began speaking. "I have six grandchildren in my house, and I have no source of income, as I am not working. I receive financial support from only some of my children, and that is not enough to feed all the mouths in this house. I run out of money well before the end of the month. Right now, I don't have a cent." Agnes paused. "I welcomed my grandchildren when their parents brought them to me, but Benedict and Prisca take months before they send any financial support. They rarely come home to visit their children. I am the one who cares for their daily needs. The mother of Benedict's children has never been here to see her kids since their divorce," said Agnes. "Oh sorry," exclaimed Aletta.

Agnes continued "Benedict is an alcoholic, and he is not prudent with his money. He should be talking to his new wife about taking custody of his children. I raised Benedict and Prisca as my kids, and now I am looking after their children as well. Who is going to take care of me? When am I going to find rest? Is this my reward for giving birth or shall I say this is my inheritance?" Agnes wrung her dry hands together as she looked at her sister in despair. "Should I be working for their children or should I go and look for employment at this age to support their children? They need books, school uniforms, medical care not to mention food and other things. Dominic and Thandi's father is living in Hartley, his hometown. Tell me, how long should I be supporting his children? Should I be the one to nag him for money for their upkeep? Dominic and Thandi came here when they were toddlers, and he has never set foot in this house or met his children; he doesn't know how grown up they are. I feel pity for these children; they are beautiful children, growing up without a father as if he is dead. At some point, I thought of taking them back to their father, but I stopped before I could do it. I thought about what people would say about that decision and how I would feel if something were to go wrong. Yes, I would feel guilty. People will point fingers at me and accuse me of neglect".

Agnes rubbed her mouth with oil before continuing "Maria came just a year ago, and she is the only one buying food for us in this house, and I can see she is trying. She pays for all our needs, but she earns less money than Prisca and Benedict. Her children are still young, and if any need arises she comes back from work to take care of it? The two boys, Bernard and Dominic, eat a lot of food and they need it because they are growing up. Several times during the day they come into the kitchen to forage for whatever food is available, and most instances there isn't any."

When Agnes stopped talking she looked relieved, it was as if she desperately needed to get all her challenges off her chest. She had spoken for over half an hour while Aletta listened patiently. Aletta could see the difficulties her sister was facing in looking after so many grandchildren without significant support from Prisca and Benedict. Aletta didn't know how to help. She became aware for the first time of her sister's grey hair and a face marked by deep wrinkles. Her tired body reflected the stresses and struggles of her life. Aletta had assumed that Agnes was faring adequately and did not need her help. To the outside world, Agnes represented a successful grandmother, one whose sons had grown up to become successful business and professional men, who were highly spoken of in Casterbridge.

Maria's eldest brother, Sylvester, following his graduation from high school, went on to become a police officer. After many years of working as a police officer, he rose through the ranks to become a deputy police commissioner. Her other brother Patrick became a teacher and the owner of three different businesses which made him one of the most successful and respected entrepreneurs in Casterbridge. Benedict became a respected industrial mechanic. Conrad started his career working in construction with local councils, and after some years he went on to become a businessman, owning some real estate properties amongst his other establishments.

The neighbours regarded Agnes highly, and some even envied her because of the success of her sons. She realised that people made judgements about her without sufficient information. Contrary to their views, Agnes saw her life through her daily challenges for bread and butter. Agnes felt that even if her sons owned flourishing businesses, her life didn't mean much if she couldn't afford a good meal before retiring to bed. If it was any consolation, she reminded her friends that her sons had their lives to lead and were family men with their responsibilities and that they supported her whenever they could.

Soon the sun disappeared below the horizon, and a fresh breeze blew from the east to dissipate the heat of the day. People drifted back from their places of business. As evening fell, the hustle and bustle of the day were replaced by a peaceful night. Bernard's shouting broke the peace, "Granny, Granny, Aunt Maria is back," as he rushed out to welcome her home.

Aletta also stood up to welcome Maria, and the two embraced each other and sat down to chat. "I heard you came back from Penrith last year and you have been busy on the market. How are you finding it?" asked Aletta.

"It was difficult when I started," replied Maria. "I learnt the ropes the hard way. Yes, indeed many times I felt like quitting, especially when my customers couldn't pay me in time, when I was robbed or when I lost money in unsaleable stock. It's not easy to describe. One has to experience it to understand fully. I made losses, but I kept trying until I got the knowledge and skills that I needed to succeed. The desire to provide for my children, as a single parent, kept me going. Every time I thought of my kids, I was moved to keeping going".

Aletta remained silent. Maria continued saying "my kids have been my inspiration, and because of them, I still stand on my own two feet and strive for something better despite all the odds against me. The first time I went into business, I didn't know where to start. I didn't have a market. I had to start to establish a market for my products, I had to fight prejudice against women, and I didn't have a source of supply. I began competing with already established people from scratch. It wasn't easy to get customers and the build loyalty. I learnt that success is something you achieve through hard work, but no one holds the candle for you through the path. However, through this business I feed my family," smiled Maria.

"How is your son? I understand he is still in Penrith?" Aletta asked.

"Mark is still in Penrith, and in three months I'll be going to fetch him," said Maria. "Now that the war is over, it should be easier for me to travel. He will be enrolled in school next year. Recently, I bought all the school books he needs."

"I feel sorry for what you went through," said Aletta. "I know it is not easy for a young woman. I'm sure you had to learn to fend for yourself quite quickly?"

"Certainly, it hasn't been easy. I realised that education is important; it helps you to make choices. I don't have any tertiary education, and so to succeed I had to keep focusing on my goal. I get up early every morning without being woken up by an alarm clock, like I used to, even when the urge to sleep one more hour is strong. No one should require an alarm clock to remind them to wake up if they are inspired with their goal. In my case, it is the welfare of my children. I want my kids to grow up and succeed. Since I started, I have not looked back or dwelt on past regrets." Maria and Aletta stayed well into the night, talking about many things until their eyes were heavy.

Some three months after Larry's letter to Maria, Matilda's health had improved significantly. The doctors had instructed her to avoid alcohol at all cost. She stopped drinking and pledged like she had done before, that she would never taste alcohol again. For weeks Matilda, repeated her pledge never taste any alcohol, to the amusement of her neighbours who were familiar with similar promises before. For weeks that followed, her body responded well to treatment, and she gained weight once again.

One weekend, Larry and Matilda were relaxing in the backyard of their house while Mark was reading his book in the house. When the doorbell rang, Mark opened it to an apparent stranger. The stranger was Maria. When Maria realised that Mark didn't recognise her, she wept. On hearing the bell, Matilda went inside and was surprised to see Maria hugging her son. Matilda was overjoyed to see her after nearly two years apart. "Welcome Maria!" she cried, taking her turn to hug Maria. "Your son is now a grown up. He can't even remember you, and I can understand why. It's been almost two years since you left Penrith. Memories fade, and people forget. Life gets busy." she consoled Maria as Mark left his mother's side to take a seat next to Matilda. "Come on, Mark, this is your mum; have you forgotten her?" Mark stared at Maria surprised, but he remained silent. He forced a smile and looked away.

Then Larry entered. "Welcome, Maria. My, but you have lost weight!" They sat down, and it was an emotional reunion as they discussed everything that had happened since the two families parted. Matilda spoke about her illness, her recovery and how Larry had to retire a few years earlier than expected to look after her. Maria told them about her life in Casterbridge and how she was managing, although her needs and the children's seemed to be growing by the day.

The next day they went down to the cemetery where Gabriel's body was buried. Larry and Matilda stood back as she came closer to Gabriel's grave. Maria wept at the memories that flooded her mind. She mouthed some words as if she expected answers to her questions, but the grave could not utter a word back. She laid some flowers and prayed for a moment. There was no one else in the cemetery at the time. Casting her eyes further down the cemetery, she noticed that there were no fresh graves, perhaps because the war had ended. Larry and Matilda were relieved when Maria re-joined them. The heat of the day was beginning to intensify. It was Matilda's first trip away from home since she came back from the hospital. She certainly needed to learn walking again after spending so many days in rehabilitation. Neither Larry nor Matilda had visited the cemetery since Gabriel's death.

Maria didn't return home with the others but went to visit her old house. There was no one at the house as the tenants were away and the gate was locked. When she got closer to her house, she could see that her house was in serious need of repairs. It was apparent that the tenants weren't taking good care of it. The outside walls were dirty; broken window panes were visible from a distance. Old and dirty curtains were hanging loosely on the windows. The gate in front of her was damaged. The flowers and fruit trees in the garden were overgrown with grass and bushes. Litter was everywhere. The enclosure around the house had been brought down. Whatever money she had received as rentals from the tenants couldn't compensate for all the repairs the house needed.

The house was the only standing achievement of her marriage to Gabriel. The dreams the two once shared were slowly fading. The idea of living the rest of their life in the house they had built was only left in imagination. The house in front of her looked ancient and dilapidated and was unlikely to be still standing in a few years to come. She could see that her children wouldn't be happy to come and live in it. This was no longer the house she had left behind nearly two years ago. She didn't have money to pay for the necessary repairs, yet in her heart, she wanted to have the house preserved. Larry was clearly not holding the tenants responsible for the damages. "Should I wait until the tenants come back so that I can complain about the condition of the house? What if they ask me to pay for the repairs?" Maria looked at the purse in her hand; the money therein was just enough to take her and Mark back to Casterbridge. As she stood in front of the gate, she became confused. She couldn't come up with any solution to address the future of the house.

Maria stood longer at the gate and kept on pondering. "Tenants don't care for what isn't theirs. They don't see their future in another person's property." She walked away disillusioned. Should she approach Larry about it and if so, what should she say? She realised she couldn't supervise the tenants' handling of the property from Casterbridge. She had to rely on Larry to collect the rent and look for new tenants whenever the property became vacant. She wondered whether she could have sold the house years earlier, but she brushed the thought aside. She said to herself "When Mark grows up he might want to come and live in his father's house. He can take with him his sisters, and they will not need to struggle for accommodation in future".

It was almost evening when she arrived at Matilda's house. Matilda had just finished preparing dinner, and they all sat around the table to eat. Matilda was an exceptional cook and that evening was no exception. Before they retired to bed, Larry said to Maria, "I received a message from Julius and Peter some months ago, alerting me that all your livestock had to be put down because of a disease. I was surprised with this news and when I went to Roselle later, their sons Joshua and Jeff told me a different story. They said that some of the livestock was sold to raise money for their needs. In other instances, their wives simply needed money for clothes and jewellery. Most of the livestock was sold within Roselle, and the money was spent on alcohol and their wives' needs. Only a single calf had died because of a disease."

Larry was embarrassed when he recounted this information. He remembered assuring Maria years earlier that all the livestock would be kept for her children. Julius and Peter had lied to Larry about visiting Maria in Casterbridge; they had never set foot there. "I am ashamed, Maria, to be telling you all this and I regret my decision. We should have sold the livestock immediately," Larry added apologetically. Maria did not respond. She had not heard from Julius and Peter for almost two years despite all the promises to visit and look after her property. Deep inside, she wondered why bad things happen to innocent and powerless people like her. It was like they had all conspired to take every means of livelihood from her. Maria realised that every promise made at the commemoration of her late husband had not been kept. "Some people pretended to be sympathetic but they are only thinking of getting something for themselves and when they get what they want they stop caring," she thought.

Larry looked at Maria again, expecting her to speak. After a while, Maria took a deep breath and said, "Larry, I have nothing to say. Whatever I will now, won't change anything. My children will just have to work harder to build their future, and they will. They will no longer have the house or the livestock to look forward to. It is a loss for me and the children, and if Mark does well in life he will build us a new house, and we will be happy again. Life is cyclical; light conquers darkness. We will come off this tragedy. I am confident he will work hard and succeed, and our lives will be better again."

Larry was surprised by Maria's answer; she spoke with such resolve and confidence as if she was prophesying the future of her children. He knew it would be many years before Mark could become a man, and for that matter be in a position to change the course of history. Larry felt the pain Maria was going through, and he quickly realised that Maria was speaking out of pain rather than confidence. Suddenly Larry shut his mouth and waited for Maria to guide the discussion.

"I went past my house, and I noticed it was in a state of disrepair," she told Larry. She described the damage and neglect she had seen. "I am sorry to hear that, Maria," Larry said apologetically. "I have not been to your house for some time since the tenant always brings the money to me here. I assumed everything was well with the house. None of the tenants has ever complained to me about the state of the house. I should indeed have found time to go and see the house, but because of Matilda's poor health, I rarely leave the house for long."

On hearing this, Maria decided against discussing the matter further with Larry as she had intended. She reasoned that if Larry had noticed the damage to the house, he would have asked the tenant to make the necessary repairs. She knew Larry had stood up for her and the children many times in the past, and he was someone she could count on when she had a problem. She wasn't prepared to burn bridges with Larry at that stage in their lives. Both of them were going through a lot, and they had supported each other in difficult times in the past. She didn't want an apology from Larry for anything. Larry obviously had his hands full because of Matilda's health, and she didn't want to make him feel bad about it, even if she was concerned about the state of her house.

Chapter 7

The hen gathers all her chicks again

After two days in Penrith Maria returned to Casterbridge; this time Mark was with her. They left early in the morning, jovially bidding farewell to Matilda and Larry. Mark was still confused why Maria was travelling with him, he knew he had not fully bonded with him, and she still appeared a stranger to him. Although Matilda had explained who Maria was, and he had understood, Mark was rather uncomfortable leaving Penrith. After travelling for a while with his mother Mark looked at Maria's face, he saw a sad person with no one to console her, and he felt sorry for her, but he didn't say anything. At that moment, Maria was pondering over the loss of her livestock, some of which had been bought with the money she earned from her poultry business. She remembered Gabriel thanking her for the money she had raised from her projects at home. When he had run short of money to conclude his livestock purchase deal, she had given Gabriel the balance from her savings. She recalled Gabriel being so grateful that Maria became determined to be an active contributor to her husband's ambition of becoming a successful farmer.

Gabriel kept a book in which he wrote down his plans for his family and in the book there was a dedicated page for each member of the family, on which he wrote his plan for each one of them. From time to time Gabriel spread these books on the table. Maria struggled to read the books as his handwriting was not easy to read, but her appreciation for Gabriel increased. She saw him as a careful planner and one of the wisest men around. Maria stole a glance at Mark, who was dozing in his seat. She saw a young lad unconcerned about any serious issues and unaware of what lay ahead.

The journey from Penrith to Casterbridge took a little more than an hour. When they arrived, Prisca was home. She had come home the previous day and would be at home for two weeks as she was on leave. She had brought new clothes for her children as well as other supplies. While Dominic and Thandi were happy that their mother had brought them gifts, the other kids were disappointed that they did not receive anything, and were apparently unhappy. Maria, on the other hand, had established a practice of buying presents for all the children without discriminating and so, whenever she bought clothes, she would buy new things for the others as well. This was what Agnes had taught her, and so she was highly regarded.

Prisca had also been taught this principle, but she had struggled to live up to it. She found it daunting and unreasonable, and she was willing to defend her decisions. Since she was rarely at home, she didn't understand the feelings of the children neither did she took any time to. For a few days, Dominic and Thandi did not play with the other kids as usual; they were dovetailing their mother wherever she went.

Agnes often had to diffuse tensions between Elizabeth and Thandi, and between Dominic and Bernard. By the end of the week, the inevitable happened when Bernard and Dominic fought over football. Prisca brought Dominic a football which he didn't want the other children to touch without his permission. While Dominic was away, Bernard went into the room where the football was kept and brought it out for all the kids to play. After they had been tired of the game, Bernard returned the ball to its place. When Dominic returned from town with his mother, he got the wind that Bernard had taken his football and was playing with it outside. This resulted in an argument with Bernard, and in anger, he smacked Bernard and the other children. Meanwhile, Agnes, who was taking a bath when this occurred, emerged to find the children in tears and Dominic still spanking Mark, his last victim. On seeing this, she flew into a rage and got into a heated exchange with Prisca who was watching the drama, as if she enjoyed Dominic disciplining the other children.

"This is my house, and none of my grandchildren should be beaten by anyone else's child, as long as I am still alive." Agnes declared angrily. "Prisca, why can't you rein in your son? Why are you watching? Why can't you stop him and take responsibility for your own child's behaviour? Answer me now!" Dominic hastily disappeared, leaving his mother being given a tongue lashing by Agnes. Prisca stood motionless as Agnes's questions rained on her. Prisca's mouth ran dry, and her lips cracked; she could not find anything to say. She knew very well that her mother resented anyone spanking the children. She was wrong not to act and restrain Dominic, and she knew she was partly to blame because of her lack of action. It was a moment of weakness with the children. She had not expected that events would turn out the way they did within a few days of arriving home. She knew if were to defend herself, it would have added more fuel to the fire. So she kept quiet and tears began to run down her cheeks. Prisca missed her children so badly when she was away and what was happening in front of her was hard to bear.

While she was still standing motionless when Agnes finished talking, Prisca remembered a similar occasion many years earlier. She had returned home complaining of a classmate who was bullying her at school and was taking her lunch box. The next day Agnes accompanied her to school. She asked to be taken to the girl, who tried running away, but Agnes caught her and took her to the headmaster. Agnes sternly cautioned the girl who was very scared and so was the headmaster. From that day, none of the school children tried to bully Prisca; they feared that she might report them to her mother.

What started as a disagreement about child conduct moved onto a discussion about living arrangements. Maria arrived at the house while Agnes and Prisca were talking. She sensed the tension and Agnes's unhappiness from the tone of her voice and decided to go straight to her room. But Agnes saw her and called her into the kitchen. Obliging, Maria came in and sat on the kitchen chair hoping that the discussion wouldn't be long. She needed to take a bath before dinner. Agnes narrated all that had occurred that afternoon while Prisca and Maria sat motionlessly. Then, she dropped a bombshell. She asked both of them to take their children away and look after them by their means.

"Your kids have parents, who are living and neither of you is handicapped. And if that is true; why you don't take your children back and look after them yourselves? I don't want to be responsible for your dependants. My house is not a permanent place for your kids. The father of your children, Prisca, is alive in Hartley. He has never been here to see his children. I am the one suffering day and night, looking after his children. Why should I carry his burdens? It is almost seventeen years now since you came back from Hartley. In all those years, I have not slept a bit because of your children. Sometimes I ask myself why I should be the one to look after her kids, while has enjoyed his life in Hartley. I have helped you enough; seventeen years is not a short time."

Turning to Maria, she said, "I know that your husband passed away and you have just been here for a short period, but even so, I want you to know that this house is not a permanent place for your children. You should look forward to moving out in the next year or so. I can't shoulder all your burdens indefinitely, and if I keep looking after your children, you will never learn and understand what is involved. It is good to shoulder your burden temporarily, but it should never be transferred to me, each has to carry their load, whether they stand or fall. You should bear the burdens and joys of being a parent alone; I can help you from a distance. I should not take that responsibility from your shoulders. I should be the one all of you are taking care of, yet none of you recognises that." Agnes paused.

Prisca and Maria knew their mother well enough to keep their mouths closed until she finished talking. When Agnes's temper had cooled, Maria stood up quietly and disappeared into her bedroom to take a bath. She was exhausted from a business day and the last things she needed at that time was a lecture from Agnes. She knew Agnes was talking from her heart because she had seen first had the struggles the high and lows of their life together since

Steps in the Middle

she relocated from Penrith, and she resonated with her feelings. She didn't want to make matter worse by responding and appearing to lessen her pain and anxieties.

Agnes's words that evening were taken seriously by both Prisca and Maria. It was true that John, Prisca's ex-husband, had neither visited nor enquired after his children, Dominic and Thandi since they had arrived in Casterbridge. John had gone on to remarry and start a new family and turned a blind eye to his children. He and Prisca had separated because of small differences. Both of them were immature at the time. John was often given to fits of anger, and when he took to laying his hands on Prisca, it was the final straw that broke the marriage. Prisca had reacted angrily and left immediately with her newborn twins.

Since that event Prisca never looked back despite the many pleas for reconciliation from John. She described the reason for her divorce as John's passionate love for dogs. He allowed them to come into the house, jump on his bed and eat from his plates. He treated dogs like they were his children. John had been raised in a family that treated dogs the same way. On the other hand, Prisca came from a family background where dogs were not allowed in the house and had specific utensils for their food and water. Dogs were strictly kept outside the house. Her family had more restrictions for dogs than John allowed.

When she married John, and they both moved into their accommodation, away from John's parents, she thought he would change. But neither of them wanted to change, and their differences became more conspicuous with time. One day, old Bailey came into the house and started feeding on a bowl of soup next to the stove. Old Bailey was one of John's oldest dogs that his late grandfather had given him. Old Bailey was a solid black

Labrador retriever, which had three puppies. When Prisca saw Old Bailey helping herself, she flew into a rage, picked up a broomstick and went hard on old Bailey. John suddenly came on the scene, and the two had an argument which led to Prisca being slapped. That was when Prisca packed her bags, took her twins and left John without any further arguments. Prisca's maintained that John loved his dogs more than her and the children whereas, John argued that his reaction was due to a temporary fit of anger.

At one point, Prisca thought about taking her children back to their father, but she feared that his new wife would ill-treat them. She also thought about the time that had elapsed since she left Hartley and she concluded that it was better that her children should stay with Agnes. The next day, Prisca was determined to talk it out with Agnes to resolve the differences between them.

"Mum," she pleaded, "I heard what you said yesterday, and I am sorry for the way things are with my life and my children. I should have made more of an effort to reconcile with John when he reached out to me. He tried for weeks; after I left him. But I was so shocked when he hit me and that I shut him out of my heart completely. It's too late now that he's married to another woman. I can't repair the damage and its water under the bridge. I regret it now. I was partly to blame. I failed to get used to treating dogs differently, and that cost me a relationship. When I look at it now, I realise my folly.

There are some things a person learns from reflection after making a mistake, which they can never go back to and correct. I learnt the hard way; I thought I was right when I left him and I was determined maintained my sense of right or wrong. I wanted to prove to him that I was right. I thought John should listen to me as his wife. I thought I could change him, but I was wrong, people are never easily changed by others. People don't want to be forced to change, and I dreamt of changing John so that he could be the man I wanted him to be. I realised later that I didn't know him well, and I misjudged him, but anyway that is now past."

Prisca gathered her thoughts before continuing. "Please help me, Mom. You gave birth to six children, and I am not one of the fortunate ones. My life has been miserable, and my children are the only consolation for my miserable life. Every day, I feel ashamed and guilty that I can't provide and support you. My life is a mess and a daily struggle. Where will I take these children to? Should I stop working, and come back and stay home? I wish life could be exchanged; I would have given up my life to someone. I am sure whoever was to take it would also have a hard time. I don't wish for anyone to have a life like mine".

"Stop right there, stop!" Shouted Agnes. "It is true mum, nothing is comfortable with my life; there are no good times. It is all one misery after another; who can cure me of this miserable life? There is always something not right in my life; I am either in a problem or out of a problem and heading towards another. These children, Dominic and Thandi, are my sole source of comfort, my hope and my reason for living. Without them why should I exist?" Prisca eyes brimmed with tears. Agnes, too, was overcome by emotion on hearing Prisca's entreaties. She broke into tears herself, and the two cried together, hugged and kissed each other.

Maria, on the other hand, told Agnes that she was ready to move out of her house along with her children. Within a short time, Maria was ready to move out. She rented a one-bedroom apartment not far from Agnes's house, and Agnes gladly gave her blessings to move out. Maria did not want a repeat of the conversation she had with Agnes. She was keen to try a new life alone with her kids. Agnes agreed that if she needed help with the children she could come back. Soon, Maria was living her life away from the oversight of Agnes. Maria's financial struggles had not ended, but she soon began to enjoy control of her life.

Mark was due to start school that month, and when she completed the enrollment process, she took him to school on his first day. Leaving her child at school was an exciting day for her. She could not hold back the tears of joy streaming down her face as she returned to her apartment. The day she had been waiting for had arrived and Mark was finally in school. Her work routine needed adjustment to accommodate her motherly role as well as Mark's school assignments. She worked half days and returned home at midday to care for her children. She taught Mark to prepare food and assigned chores to each child to perform in the apartment every day, a function she had learnt from Agnes. Every afternoon Maria checked that each task had been done to her satisfaction.

Within a few weeks of training, Maria's children learnt how to work without supervision. Mark was able to cook and look after his sisters while Maria was away. She encouraged Mark to read in the afternoon which helped him perform better at school and obtain good grades. Maria arranged with Mark's teacher to keep her informed of his progress. She was particularly interested in updates regarding his understanding, comprehension and writing skills. She prepared Mark in advance to give him an edge over other school children. Reading sessions with Mark went on every day after school. Maria was so enthusiastic about the success of her son that she never got tired of helping him with school assignments.

One day, after returning from work at midday, and after a short while she went out to meet some neighbours. She didn't expect to be out long, but the unexpected happened, she ended up staying longer than she had planned. When she left, Mark was having lunch with his sisters. On the table were Mark's books, which he was meant to read that afternoon. But then, his school friend Bothwell came to visit him holding a football. Bothwell invited Mark to play outside, and he obliged. Mark left his books on the table and without thinking very much went outside to enjoy football with his friend.

When Maria returned home and found Mark playing with his buddy outside, she hauled him back to the table where his books were, escorted Bothwell to the gate and asked him to leave immediately. From that day Bothwell never came back to Maria's apartment while Maria was present. He would first peep through a crack in the wall surrounding the apartment to check whether Maria was there. Both the boys were scared of Maria. Her stern warning to Mark was never forgotten. Maria often insisted that Mark carries out his reading assignment before lunch. Mark struggled to read at first but gradually improved with Maria's help.

Meanwhile, Agnes's life didn't change much since Maria left, except that the number of children in her house had been reduced to four. She still sat on her patio watching them playing. She felt happy that she had lived long enough to see her children grow up, and have their families. She felt privileged that her sons ranked among the well-known business people in Casterbridge. Sylvester had bought the house she was living in over twenty years ago. Patrick and Conrad took turns every month to send her supplies and pay her bills and often came to visit her with their families. As Agnes reflected on her life and the lives of her children, she realised that she had privileges which other women of her age were longing for. Yes, there was much in her life to be thankful for. Things were not as dismal as she sometimes thought. She smiled and lifted her hands to the heavens in gratitude.

Agnes's house was large and attractive with its tiled roof. Its location at the corner of a quiet street made it clearly visible. People often used it as a reference point when giving directions. Many senior women in her community envied her. "Although my life has not been that rosy, I have never gone hungry for a day," she thought. "I have one of the most attractive houses in this area so I shouldn't be unhappy. Why do I sometimes think my life is miserable?"

Agnes began to see another side to the story of her life. She had always been worried about what she didn't have and would be obsessed with this until she eventually got what she wanted. She complained about her situation to every one of her children who would care to listen. Agnes mused, "I must stop complaining about what I don't have but rather focus my mind of the kind things my sons are doing for me. I must be more appreciative and grateful about this. I am one of the most fortunate senior women in this community. Many other women of my age have not even seen their grandchildren, but I have. Others don't have sons who pay their bills and yet mine do. I should stop being unhappy; sometimes they delay payments, but eventually, all bills do get paid. My sons are family men; they also have their children, and I need to change the way I talk to them."

Agnes felt a new sense of pride, and suddenly she felt new energetic rushing in her body. "Why am I feeling relieved? If it is true that I am one of the most privileged women in Casterbridge, why weren't I seeing it all along? Why did it take so long to realise? Is this an illusion? Is my assessment correct? Why am I seeing it now, yet nothing has changed since yesterday? Could it be true that my past behaviour has been responsible for my unhappiness? Do I have control over how I respond to things happening in my life? Was I not responsible for my action a few months ago when I spoke angrily to Maria and Prisca? I think I was, but I am old enough to make changes to the way I respond to events. I can choose not to be miserable. I can opt to be polite and control my anxieties. Perhaps my blood pressure would even be better. I can keep my temper from flaring up by focusing my mind on the beautiful things in my life. My life isn't that bad after all," Agnes said to herself as she walked around her garden.

By midday, Agnes's grandchildren arrived with their school report cards in hand. As she sat on her favourite couch in the living room, each grandchild came and gave her their school report card to read. She watched them all as they filed past her, after which they proceeded to their rooms to change their uniforms before seating around the kitchen table for lunch. Within a few minutes the boys were quarrelling in the kitchen over food, and soon a fight broke.

Agnes's emotions were immediately stirred, and she immediately thought of marching to the kitchen, to deal decisively with the combatants but her dress was caught up in the arms of the couch, and she couldn't release it. By the time she managed to disentangle her dress from the couch nail, the quarrelling and fighting had already been diffused by Thandi and Elizabeth, so Agnes didn't even bother to go to the kitchen. She remained seated on her couch and remembered that she had committed herself to staying calm and avoiding over-reacting. She reflected on how quickly her temper had flared when she heard the noise in the kitchen and how she was determined to march into the kitchen and bring the screaming to an end. Agnes realised that if she was going to succeed in changing her life, it was going to take some adjustments before she could achieve that goal. There would be no quick solutions; she would need to replace her old habits with new ones. The boys' quarrel in the kitchen was a test of how much she still needed to work on herself. Agnes laughed at herself. "I would never have thought about this if my dress had not been caught up by the couch. Sometimes I need to be quick to react but slow to anger."

The report cards were still on the table. When she looked at them, all she could see were different colours. "What do these report cards mean?" she asked herself. "I didn't attain any education that much, and I am just a poor old soul who can't read." She looked again at the report. "Dominic!" she called. Dominic came running, and Bernard also came in. "Can you read the report for me?" she asked.

Dominic took the first report and said:

"This is Thandi's report." He stopped. "Go on," Agnes demanded. Dominic remained silent, and Bernard who was standing nearby snatched the report from Dominic. Dominic was embarrassed, and seething with anger, he walked out of the room, and he went to watch the proceedings through the window. He didn't want his report to be read by Bernard, but Bernard carried on eloquently reading the reports for Agnes who sat quietly in front of him.

Agnes was practising to control her emotions, and from that day she became aware of Dominic's reading difficulties. In fact, when Bernard read Dominic's report card, Dominic listened carefully through the window, and that was the first time Dominic also understood what was written on his report card. He had never been able to read the report himself nor comprehend it. The report stated that Dominic had failed all the subjects and the teacher's was requesting a meeting with Dominic's parents.

Steps in the Middle

Next, Bernard picked his report card and read it to Agnes. He had done well in all his studies and in fact was the third best pupil in his class. Agnes stood up and hugged him, and gave him a pat on his shoulders, much to the amusement of Bernard. Both Thandi and Elizabeth's report cards were the same; both had a mediocre performance, and their teachers had commented that they could do better by reading and practising at home. When Bernard finished reading the report cards, Agnes called all the children inside and tried to explain the importance of school. They all listened intently, but she could not tell whether they took it to heart. Agnes, who was training herself to control the way she reacted to things, hugged each one before dismissing them. Afterwards, she felt a sense of gratitude that she had learnt something about herself that day and her grandchildren.

Chapter 8

The road from St. Columbus

Maria arrived at St. Columbus Mission the following day, and Aletta took her straight into a small meeting room where three nuns were already seated. Aletta left as she was not involved in the interview process. Maria, having never been interviewed for a job, was nervous. But she must have answered the question satisfactorily as the nuns agreed to hire her on a three-month trial period, after which they would assess her performance. Maria was delighted, and after thanking the nuns, she broke the news to Aletta who immediately offered a prayer.

As she went on her way home, she wondered how she was going to manage to look after the kids while working away from home. She had become reliant on Mark's help when she was away, but how would she be able to supervise Mark's school assignments? There was also her business to consider, which gave her an income and the freedom to come back home when she needed to. On the other hand, earnings from her business were unpredictable? Should she continue to struggle in a mostly male-dominated sector? "Perhaps, I should have asked for some more time before accepting the job offer. Maybe, this is the only chance I have to enter into formal employment and earn a fixed, regular income." She thought.

She continued to debate with herself on the merits of a regular income as against self-employment. If she were to choose a job at St. Columbus, she would miss her children, and they would have to go back and live with Agnes again. Her children would grow up in her absence, missing her like they already missed their father.

"Is that what I want? But if I refuse the job, I will continue to struggle with irregular and unpredictable income. Miss this chance at your peril!" she told herself. "This is my only opportunity to get into formal employment. I have no professional skills and what better can I get than this. I will be part of an organisation with fringe benefits, which means I can change my life and give my children a better future". Maria was also troubled by having to go back and ask for help from Agnes. She had just moved out of Agnes's house, not so long ago.

The bus taking her back to Casterbridge passed a large recreational park, with well-maintained lawns and pathways, flanked by flowering rose bushes leading to a fountain. Maria gazed in wonder at the gardens where visitors sat on benches, engrossed in their conversations with some reading books quietly. Further down the park, she noticed a couple reclining on a rug spread on the lawn, holding hands and kissing. On seeing this from the bus window, Maria began to reminisce about her love life, remembering that she had once felt this way for Gabriel; when she couldn't spend a day without him.

A few feet away from the lovers, she saw another couple watching over their two children, a boy and a girl, running around the park area. Maria was reminded of one Sunday when she and Gabriel went to the park in Penrith with their children, that was shortly after they relocated from Roselle. The kids were overjoyed, playing on the swings until they were tired and hungry. After eating the sandwiches she had prepared for them, they fell all asleep. She and Gabriel had to carry them and their bikes back home.

When Maria arrived in Casterbridge, she went straight to the home of Florence Kiff, Mark's school teacher. They had become close friends not only through their mutual interest in Marks's progress but also because they were once classmates at the same school years earlier. Maria subsequently dropped out of school during her junior academic years, after her third grade. The two were reunited when Maria started supplying vegetables to the school Florence was a teacher. It took Maria some time to build the trust with the school before she started receiving regular orders. It was then that Florence and Maria met again.

Florence admired Maria for her business skills and industriousness. She saw her as a courageous woman, who had managed to break into a male-dominated sector against all the odds. She always doubted whether she would be able to quit her job and start a business like Maria. On the other hand, Maria considered Florence as very educated and successful. She respected and trusted Florence, and wished she had a job like Florence's. Maria always admired school teachers, as she thought the only worked half a day and then spent the rest of the afternoon playing sports with school children. She felt it was a satisfying and easy job, which she could manage if she had the education.

When she arrived at Casterbridge primary school, Maria had

Steps in the Middle

one thing in mind; she wanted to open up and confide with Florence. She was convinced that Florence would be able to give her sound advice. Florence understood that Maria had just accepted a job offer at St Columbus orphanage as an assistant, working with children. She clearly displayed her excitement for taking up the offer and proceeded to explain that she would be paid a fixed monthly salary, giving her the security of a full-time job which was less strenuous than being self-employed. After explaining everything, she asked Florence for her honest opinion.

Florence was taken aback as she had never spoken to Maria on personal matters, only about Mark's education, other trivial matters and placing orders for vegetables. She began, "Thanks, Maria. I feel honoured in the trust you have put on me to help you with your personal matter. It is a delicate matter, and my view is a personal one and may not be right for you. So don't feel obliged to follow my advice."

She looked at Maria. "It seems that you are looking for a change in your career, a job that gives you more time to rest, less strain and would provide a regular salary. Is my understanding correct?" Maria nodded in agreement. Her thoughts were running through the opportunities her new employment would bring her. She expected Florence to affirm her decision to take full-time employment. She had chosen self-employed because that was the only option she had been experienced in while she was in Penrith.

"There is a world of difference between self-employment and working for an organisation. When you are self-employed, you have control over your life, working hours and income, whereas when you are employed on a job, you get paid a fixed amount often restricted by contract. Your income as an entrepreneur is limited only by your imagination, and you are your master.

Working for someone earns you a salary and gives you a standard of living. In my case, the salary is just enough to take me from one month to another, and this has created a vicious circle that I am struggling to escape. Each time I see you come to our school to deliver an order, I feel inspired to want to be like you, but I don't have the guts to take the leap of faith into entrepreneurship. Entrepreneurship provides you with a chance to build wealth, and no one has ever gotten rich because of working on a job. You have more skills for growing a business than I have, yet you think what I have is preferable." Florence paused.

"I want to emphasise that you're never going to get rich by working for a salary," Florence continued. "You are already a success in my eyes, and you are on the right path to your financial freedom. We all feel like quitting at some stage, and I understand the stress you are going through. Don't throw away the diamond you have in your hand because you have been waiting so long to have it polished. Sometimes, I feel I am not being appreciated in my job. As an employee, you will be bound by rules of employment and so will be your reward. Compliance with the rules of employment will earn you approval by the employer. You have limits to try new things and often you need to seek approval at every stage. After many years of studying at university, some people end up regretting that they never developed their talent in a field they enjoy. This is because many are often persuaded by parents, friends or academic institutions to pursue courses which they never actually like. So when they finish their course, they sense a void, caused by not pursuing their passion."

Florence recounted the experience of Dr John Halford who lived near Casterbridge. His loving parents raised him; his father was a medical doctor and his mother a dentist. When John finished high school, his parents took him to Boston Medical School where he graduated at the top of his class, much to the delight of his parents. He returned to set up a private practice in Casterbridge and soon became a respected specialist. After ten years at the pinnacle of his career, he took his parents by surprise when he told them that he was going to Texas, to pursue his passion for fish farming. They were stunned and disappointed. They tried to persuade him otherwise, as did his friends. But John paid no notice, and he proceeded to leave it all. Within three years, he built a company that supplied fish in all Casterbridge.

"Find your passion and pursue it," said Florence. "Don't take up a job until you have thought through everything. Sometimes you may not know what you have until you've lost it, and in some instances, your provision may reside in your problem, and therefore don't quit your business easily, you may be close to your breakthrough. This new opportunity may look appealing to you because you are feeling stressed, yet the solution to your stress may be resolved by taking time off rather than a change of profession. Check whether what you want to do is in harmony with your greater goal and make your decision carefully. Like it is said, the grass is always greener on the other side."

A knock on Florence's door interrupted the conversation. It was her husband. He walked in and greeted Maria before proceeding into his bedroom. It was now dark outside when Florence accompanied Maria out of her house. When they parted Florence said, "You still have three weeks before you start and if you decide against accepting the offer, there is enough time to notify St Columbus." The two parted quietly.

Florence had taken Maria to a place inside her heart where she was afraid to go alone. As she lay awake that night, she pondered her options again. It was clear that Florence didn't affirm her choice as she expected. She remembered a similar situation years earlier when she and Gabriel stayed awake all night while deciding on a job offer. Now she was facing a similar situation alone. The way Florence looked at her situation was an eye-opener for her. She knew Florence was right about self-employment but somehow, she started feeling unsure about her judgement. Florence's words kept playing in her head and she could hear her saying, "Employment gives you a fixed income and a standard of living, but entrepreneurship lets you build your wealth. No one gets rich because of employment." Maria had never perceived what she was doing as being entrepreneurial.

Later that night, she began doubting Florence's assessment. "If it were correct, why would Aletta have forgotten to mention this important fact, if she knew I was capable of becoming wealthy in my own business?" Maria began to discount Florence's assessment, feeling that she had no knowledge of how she was struggling, and hence she spoke from her perception of how Maria was faring, and not the reality that Maria was living.

But what if Florence was right? Can another person recognise the potential in another individual, which the individual can't notice by themselves? Sometimes, talented Individuals find it easy to discount their talent, resulting in them failing to develop their fully potential, until someone they respect convinces them to. Maria was focusing on her financial needs at hand; her primary concern was a stable income and less physical strain. Accordingly, she saw full-time employment was a panacea for her problems. She reasoned that if she worked hard in her new job, she would make her organisation proud, and in time her salary would be increased.

Meanwhile, Agnes didn't know that Maria had gone to St Columbus; and that she had already been interviewed and had accepted the job offer. When Maria finally told Agnes the news, Agnes was delighted for Maria's sake, but at the same time, she didn't think it was a good idea. She didn't want Maria to accept the job because it meant her kids would be back in her house. The struggle of providing for grandchildren, whose parents were not responsible, had left an indelible impression on her heart. Agnes already had enough trouble looking after Prisca and Benedict's children. She didn't want to express the same thoughts openly to Maria. Agnes was good at presenting a straight face, and even though Maria had stayed with her for many years, she still didn't know what Agnes was thinking.

On the other hand, Agnes loathed disappointing Aletta, whose help had opened up the opportunity for Maria to get a job. It was all very complicated. Maria, on her part, sensed that Agnes wasn't happy with her decision to take the offer. She had great respect for Florence, Agnes and Aletta, but the feeling of disappointing Aletta was stronger than all other justifications for not taking the job. After a while, Maria began to veer towards not accepting the job offer, but the fear of disappointing Agnes and Aletta was overpowering. For several days, Maria teetered between two opinions.

Chapter 9

The day they knew who they were

After three weeks, the matter was resolved. Maria departed for St. Columbus leaving her children with Agnes. Bernard progressed well academically, and at the end of the year he graduated from junior school with good grades and was ready to go to high school. His father, Benedict, was impressed with his examination results. He decided to enrol him at a school in Southwark, the town where he was employed. Thus Benedict and Bernard could stay together. Benedict's apartment was within walking distance from Bernard's school.

Thandi and Dominic had graduated a year early, and while Thandi continued her high school education in Casterbridge, Dominic, who had failed dismally every class, decided to try other avenues. He persuaded Agnes to allow him to look for employment or to take a vocational course. Agnes did not object to Dominic's idea, although she wasn't familiar with vocational courses. Elizabeth also graduated and proceeded to high school in Casterbridge, and Benedict's new wife agreed to look after her. So Elizabeth moved out of Agnes's house and went to live with her stepmother. It was difficult for her at first, but in time she began to feel more comfortable as her stepmother treated her fairly.

On the other hand, Bernard was not happy staying with his father in Southwark. Benedict had drifted into an alcoholic. Bernard's struggles were not apparent to his step mother who lived in their family home in Casterbridge. On some occasions, Benedict would leave for work in the morning and wouldn't return home until two or three days later, causing his son untold worry. Bernard felt powerless to confront his father. The situation deteriorated further with Benedict failing to provide for Bernard until he was forced to meet his uncle Conrad to discuss the matter. Conrad agreed to allow Bernard to move in with his family. When Conrad confronted Benedict about the plight of his son, he became evasive at first, but with more pressure on him, Conrad was able to get an admission he needed. The two discussed and agreed that Benedict would continue paying school levies for his son, while Conrad would provide him with accommodation and food.

It didn't take long for Benedict to break the agreement. Within a few months, Benedict couldn't keep up with payments. Bernard was disappointed with his father's failure to pay his school levies as well as his reluctance to visit him. Years before, Benedict had always argued that he didn't have enough time to travel to Casterbridge to visit his family, but things didn't change when Bernard move in with Conrad's family. Conrad lived in Claremont, less than thirty minutes' bicycle ride away. Benedict didn't work weekends, most of which he spent in nightclubs dotted around his suburb. He regularly enjoyed drinking beer with his friends until his purse was empty. His bills steadily accumulated and would remain unpaid until he was hauled to courts or services were disconnected. His failure to pay bills wasn't due to shortage of funds but the allocation of it. While he was very generous in buying drinks at the nightclub, his generosity was not the same at home. Benedict's wife took it upon herself to provide for her children without any help from him. He would occasionally travel to Casterbridge, and on his way back, Benedict regularly pleads with Agnes to lend him money for his ticket back to Southwark. Each time he borrowed money from Agnes, he would promise to pay back as soon as possible, but he seldom did. His failure to honour his word did little to improve relations with Agnes, and subsequently with the rest of his brothers.

One autumn, Conrad drove Agnes and his family to Hartley where they had been invited to a wedding party. Prisca arrived early as did Maria, Patrick and Sylvester. Benedict was also present. With music playing in the background, guests took to dancing and so did the bride and groom. Many guests brought gifts and personally delivered them to the bride and groom. Benedict stood up from the crowd, took out his purse and donated the entire contents, much to the applause of everyone at the party. Benedict made himself a spectacle of the party when he took to drinking beer, which was freely served during the party. He danced to the lively music, with his glass of beer in one hand and swinging one end of the arena to another before receiving a standing ovation. His unrestrained dance pushed his brothers to the edge; they could not wait for the event to come to an end.

Benedict siblings were relieved when the festivities were over. As guests began leaving, Benedict realised that he had no money for his bus ticket back to Southwark. He sobered up, walked briskly to Agnes who was now seated in Conrad's car and ready to leave, knelt beside the car window and begged Agnes for money. Agnes said firmly, "I don't have money, Benedict! As you can see, Conrad is the one who brought me here, and he is now taking me back home. Why don't you ask for help from him?" Conrad, who was already in his car, was not familiar with Benedict's theatrics. When he saw Benedict kneeling outside the window, he felt embarrassed and outraged. Seething with anger, his hands shaking violently, he extracted a note from his purse and threw it in Benedict's face. He drove off leaving Benedict kneeling on the ground. Benedict rose from the ground, dusted himself and pick up the note and was on his way to Southwark. Not many people at the event saw the drama unfolding as everyone was busy making their preparations to leave.

Conrad was angry all the way to Casterbridge. "This is humiliating, Mother. I look after Benedict's son in Southwark. He neither visits nor financially supports him, but he has time to travel many miles away for a party. He had money for a gift at the wedding, but he has no money for his son's school levy or clothes. Now, he has the audacity to borrow money for his bus ticket back to Southwark. I am very disappointed with his behaviour." Conrad banged his hand against the steering wheel, as the car sped away from Hartley. Agnes and Beauty remained quiet until Conrad's anger had receded. Agnes said, "What you have seen is just the tip of an iceberg. Benedict hasn't been home for the past three months, and he hasn't sent a single cent to his wife. She came to my house a few days ago crying like a baby. She told me she had no food for the children and I told her that I could help them too. I advised her to go to Southwark and discuss her problems with Benedict."

Conrad said, "Mother, Bernard came to me and told me he hadn't eaten anything for nearly three days, and he didn't know what to do. Bernard is his son, and he is still young, and so Benedict should take his family responsibility seriously. It is time for him to get the message loud and clear. I gave him money only because you were with me; otherwise, I wouldn't have. He is an adult, and he should learn to behave like one."

Conrad and Agnes parted but the events of that day were imprinted on his mind. Conrad understood only too well why Bernard struggled to live with his father. He recalled that one of Benedict's friends had become an alcoholic. As the saying goes, birds of a feather flock together and, like his buddies, Benedict sunk deeper into alcohol addiction by the day.

With the growth of the economy in Casterbridge, Patrick's retail business thrived, his sales doubled, and he responded by expanding the supermarket staff. When Dominic dropped out of school, Patrick offered him a job as a cashier at his supermarket, and he accepted. Within a few weeks, he commenced his training and not only was he handling the work without supervision but he developed excellent relations with the customers. Dominic's superb customer service attracted a lot of respect and praise colleagues and customers alike, and this set him for high responsibility in the business.

Mark, Martha and Masculine did well at school, and their reports were consistently better. With Dominic now employed, household income increased and life became much easier for Agnes and her grandchildren. Maria visited home only occasionally, usually unexpectedly, much to the surprise of Agnes and her children. However, she regularly sent supplies for her children, and this she thought compensated in part, for her extended period of absence from home. However, it was difficult for her to participate in their school activities and the children had to do without her as best as they could. When funds were required urgently at school, Maria had to be summoned from St Columbus which was time-consuming and challenging for her and the children.

With time the children became accustomed to her prolonged absence from home. Consequently, Maria missed out on many crucial moments in her children's lives which she could have celebrated with them, such as when they brought their annual school reports cards, or when they moved upwards from one class to the next. The next time she would be home on leave, the children would forget to tell her about these precious moments they had while she was away, because often the moments would have been surpassed by events or would have become irrelevant by then. The short time that Maria would be home on leave made it difficult for her to connect with the children and she would at times appear strange and disconnected to them. Agnes became the foster mother of Maria's children, and whenever Maria was home, she would update her with all the day-to-day events in their lives as best as she could remember.

Every year, parents were invited to come to the school to discuss their children's performance with their teachers. Agnes never attended school meetings, and so when Mark, Martha and Masculine were asked where their father was, Mark told the teacher that he had died some years earlier. The teacher asked him, "So you are orphans?"

He replied, "Yes sir."

"Who pays your school levy?" asked the teacher.

"My mother, she works at St Columbus," Mark replied.

"I am sorry to hear that."

The teacher ordered the children to go home since there were no classes that day. Mark, Martha and Masculine were the only children dismissed as all the others had their parents ready to meet their teachers. As they walked away from the school hall, Mark and his sisters realised that as orphans they were different from other school children. They wished their mother was there to stand up for them. Before this episode; Maria had always shielded them from this experience.

When Mark's friend, Bothwell, saw the three walking out the school hall, he ran up and asked,

"Where are you going, Mark? Why didn't you bring your mother?"

"My mum is at St Columbus, and the teacher said we are orphans so we should go back home since we don't have parents to meet our teachers," Mark replied.

Bothwell felt sorry for Mark and his sisters, and he shook his head in sympathy before running back into the school hall. Mark saw that Martha was crying and Masculine appeared confused about what the teacher had told them. He tried to comfort them as they walked away.

"I will tell Mom, and next time she will come. Don't worry Martha. Let us go home and tell Grandma."

Mark held the hands of his sisters as they walked away from the school premises and he too was feeling very sorrowful. The teacher's questions that day brought to the fore something about their life they had never confronted head-on. The three had never viewed themselves as orphans, although no doubt they had heard Agnes using the term when talking to a friend. "So, it is true that we are orphans," Mark said to himself.

"The teacher has just told us, and every school child has seen us being dismissed for the day because we don't have parents."

When they got home, Mark told Agnes what had happened, and Agnes explained the meaning of the word. It was the first time that Mark and his sisters were confronted with the difficulty of being an orphan. Being an orphan became the reason why they didn't have all the books, they were treated differently and so on and so forth. They started looking out for instances when they were left out and analysing the reasons given. With time, the three became much closer. Mark would stand up for his sisters whenever he saw them being affected by any event at home or school, in which they were being discriminated. The way they saw themselves changed; all along they had thought they were like other children.

Some children were curious enough to ask Masculine, "What happened to your father? Where is he and where is your mother? Is she dead also?" Masculine, who was born after Gabriel had passed on, had no idea of what the discussion was about. Having been born in the absence of Gabriel, the talk about a father didn't impact her until later. She would become irritable when questions were asked about her father and in some instances would fight other girls. Mark intervened to help his sisters deal with the absence of Gabriel and Maria. He asked them to report anyone who made remarks about their family situation. As time progressed, Mark realised how vulnerable he and his sisters were to bullying by other old children. He realised that it was up to him to protect and stand up for them when Agnes was not available. Mark acquired maturity beyond his years and neighbours noticed his good behaviour and respected him.

On Christmas day, when Agnes and her grandchildren walked to church, the neighbours' children were clad in new clothes.

Mark and her sisters did not, and that meant they were reluctant to play with other kids to avoid being mocked because of their old clothes. At the conclusion of the mass, they all followed Agnes back home in a single file instead of going to play in the Cathedral grounds as they would normally do. Mark was sad when he saw his friend Bothwell, his sister and other children enjoying themselves, and the day became unpleasant for him. He noticed that his sisters were also hurting when suddenly a little girl called out,

"Masculine, where is your new dress? Go and get your dress and come to play!"

Masculine walked off indignantly without a word. Agnes, who was wearing a new dress that Sylvester had bought for her that week, must have heard the little girl and sensed the tension in the air. She could not help the situation, as she relied on financial support from her sons. Thandi was not with them; she had been invited to spend Christmas at her uncle's place.

When they got home, Mark assured his sisters that their mother would send them new clothes. But that did nothing to cheer them up. They all looked miserable and sad, feeling that no one cared for them. Mark knew his mother loved them, and that she was the only hope they had of ever getting new clothes, but the pain of living without her was equally distressing. They knew she was a single parent and they were orphans. He realised that their life was different from that of other children, with both parents and he began ways of limiting the difficulties of not living with Maria. One thing that kept bothering him was the realisation that there were the last to get Christmas clothes and the last to get school levies paid and so on.

Mark and his sisters stopped visiting their friends' houses because they didn't want to explain anything regarding their family situation. From time to time Bothwell and his sisters would come to Agnes's house to play, bringing toys so that all of them would enjoy time together. When they were done, Bothwell would collect all his toys and load them into a box before going home. This was because Bothwell preferred to exchange toys rather than loan them. It was as though he controlled their happiness; when he came with toys and took them when he left.

After a while, Mark began to attract the attention of older people because of his humility and decorum. He spoke with sincerity and maturity. At home, Mark assigned tasks to his sisters every day, taught them to cook and perform other more important household chores. Agnes was impressed and trusted him to carry out tasks unsupervised, even as far as delivering messages and making payments to her accounts. With this added responsibility Mark's school work also improved and his teacher commented on his good behaviour.

One day, Mark was sitting outside the house when he saw Bothwell's father passing by. He heard him telling Bothwell, who was riding a bike,

"Be careful, there's a car coming!"

Mark thought about the words Bothwell's father had uttered, and he perceived him as a kind father who cared for his children and that Bothwell and his siblings were very privileged to have such a father. He wished he also had a father who would tell him, "Be careful, there is a car coming!" Mark knew then that it would be up to him to assume the role of a caring father for his sisters. His sisters needed someone to protect them and stand up for them to provide protection against bullying. From that day, Mark further strengthened his resolve to ensure that no one would harm or bully his sisters.

Mark needed a father figure to act as a role model, to mentor him and answer some questions he had in his mind. His sisters had Agnes to respond to their girl questions, but Mark had no one. In quiet moments alone he cried over this lack of support. He would walk to the park near Agnes' house and sit down, and for hours he would think about life's questions and make resolutions regarding his future. People admired his confidence, early maturity and self-discipline, yet inside he felt alone with no one to turn to. Mark began to spend a lot of time alone thinking about his life and the life of his sisters. He wondered how he could change their lives, how he could stop people from looking down upon them as orphans but rather look at them as any other children with a bright future. He wondered what it was he could do to change their social status. As he dwelt on his current circumstances rather than the prospects, he realised it would be many years before he was able to transform his life.

Every school vacation, Mark would spend most vacations with his sisters at Agnes house. His friend Bothwell and his parents occasionally travelled on holiday and would not be back until the end of the vacation. Many times, he pondered over how he and his sisters ever going to travel anywhere on vacation.

"When Bothwell comes back, he will tell me what they did in Southwark and other places, but I won't have anything new to tell him. Last school term, my teacher asked each pupil to tell the class where they had travelled to, and I was embarrassed to say I hadn't gone anywhere. How I wish to tour with my family and see new places and take pictures to show my friends and my teacher," Mark thought to himself, feeling distraught.

"When I grow up, I want to be a businessman. I want to build houses and properties so that I can provide people with affordable accommodation and travel to different places. I want to work hard and buy a car and a house in a big town like Southwark for my mother and sisters."

Mark must have shouted his thoughts aloud when Robert Wood, who lived a few blocks away from Agnes's house, called out, "Who are you talking to?" Mark stopped and utterly surprised that someone was looking at him, looked at Mr Wood and smiled. "I was soliloquising," he said as he smiled.

Mr Wood didn't smile back, he looked worried, and he replied, "Wait, I want to talk to you, son." Mr Wood was a quiet and well-respected man with grown up sons and daughters. Mark felt flattered by Mr Wood calling him 'son'. No one had ever called him this way before, and the word 'son' made him feel loved and endeared. He crossed over the road from where he was standing at the bus stop.

"You must be having a lot on your mind to be talking to yourself like that. Am I correct?" Mr Wood enquired looking at Mark straight in his eyes.

Mark looked away shyly. He remained silent opting to avoid revealing his thoughts. Mr Wood's saw through his hesitancy and put his hand on his shoulder. "I am familiar with what children go through when they lose one or both parents. You can feel isolated and at a loss of who to confide in," he whispered. "I was a businessman before, buying and selling farm produce in and around Casterbridge and my wife was a full-time mother working from home. One day my wife collapsed and died soon after I left home one morning. I got the message when I was at work, and I came back immediately, and after three days she was buried. I stopped working full time, and I came back home to look after my children. In the early days of the loss, my sons and daughters appeared to cope very well with the death. Consequently, I thought we had crossed the valley and were ready to move on. After two years, my daughters began struggling to cope with the death of their mother, and I had to arrange to counsel for them. I am sure you miss your mum, and you probably miss your father as well. Don't be shy about it; it happens. It's not your fault. When was your mother last home?" Mr Wood asked.

"About five months ago," Mark replied.

"I know you are still very young and you may feel shy to say how you feel about what's going on in your life. You may have questions and worries, but be assured everything will be all right at some stage. You will grow up to become a man, but you must continue to be disciplined, focused on your future and not the past. If you regularly look at the past, you will lose energy to move forward. Often the past doesn't determine destiny; it is just a footprint of where you have been and a testimony of your footprints before reaching your present position. Your loss is now history and history doesn't change. But you can still change where you are going, and the future is a dream to be grasped by those who keep their hopes alive. Keep looking at the future; don't blink, because if you do, you might miss to taking note milestones that you have come. Don't listen to cynics and ridiculers, they always predict doomsday, and they will always be there. Don't be mistaken and don't be confused, the job of a ridiculer is to ridicule. Don't wish the ridiculer doesn't ridicule you; that will be a terrible mistake to make, but hope that the ridiculer does ridicule and you keep moving on. Keep focusing on your future, what you want to achieve, and work day and night for the change in life that you want to see. You can't move mountains in a day, but you can carry one stone at a time. You must work hard and read your

Steps in the Middle

books and have a vision of what you want to achieve and see," he paused.

Mr Wood paused again before continuing, "Don't be shy because you can't afford certain things today, but keep your hope alive that tomorrow will be better than today. Keep telling yourself it will be all right one day and certainly it will be, one day. At times you may have to keep reassuring yourself even if you are hurting inside or have tears on your face. You will grow up to be successful, and you will be able to look after your mother and do whatever you want." By this time they had crossed the road and were both sitting on a bench at the bus stop. No one else was around.

"Do you hear me?" Mr Wood continued. "Don't worry that your mother is not living with you and don't worry if people call you orphans. It doesn't change anything in your life. Your time will come when life will be in your favour. Most importantly, don't fight anyone and don't feel sorry for yourself. Don't think you are a victim; tragedy happens to all of us, you lost your father, and I lost my wife, is there any better loss? Ask yourself every day one question: what can I do today to make my future bright, because you can still re-arrange your day tomorrow. The past is buried, and you can do nothing about it. If you do what I am telling you every day and keep working on yourself, your future will be brighter than the sun, and you will be happy today despite turmoil around you because you keep your focus on the possibilities of tomorrow," said Mr Wood waving his hands.

"Don't let the comments of ridiculer get inside your heart, always keep the bad and the unpleasant outside, and if you manage to do that, you will be happy. A ship can float free in high seas as long as it doesn't allow the water around it to get inside it, yet it needs the water to reach its destination. Cynics and ridiculers should inspire you to work harder to be better so that you can prove them wrong. I already see a bright future for you." Mr Wood paused.

Mark remained speechless, he wasn't sure he understood everything Mr Wood had spoken, but he was sure his words were what he desperately needed. There was a moment of silence as the words sank into Mark's heart. Mr Wood seemed to speak in riddles, and Mark couldn't decipher the meaning of some of the statements.

"Ponder about the things I have told you and if you need us to talk further, come to my house," said Mr Wood. Just then, the bus came, and Mr Wood stood up and hopped on. The bus departed down the street while Mark remained standing on the spot. Mr Wood appeared to have read his mind apparently. "Was it easy to read other people's minds or he was just guessing? How did he know what I was thinking" Marked mused over events of the moments past? Mark found Mr Wood respectful, and he felt the love and compassion in his voice. "Mr Wood is an eloquent speaker, and I like the way he stressed his words," he thought. Mark began to idealise Mr Wood as his role model. He wished Mr Wood was his father. "I need a man to talk to, someone who understands a boy without a father. I need someone who is available for me every day when I come home from school. I need someone who can teach me to be a strong man and become a father like him."

Mark cast his eyes down the road, but the bus was no longer in sight. He wished Mr Wood had more time to talk to him. He enjoyed the conversation although he didn't want to answer. He was shy and insecure. He was afraid to open up. He feared that if he were to tell him how he felt, Mr Wood would share the information with others. "I wish he would take me where he was going," Mark yearned. "All right, I must go home and be locked behind the gate until the school vacation ends," Said Mark as he walked away from the bus stop.

While Mark was walking home, he remembered how Bothwell was very close to his father. "It is a privilege to have a father. I wish I had one. I would call him Dad like Bothwell does. I would ask him the questions every boy wants to know when I come back from school," Mark thought as he reached home.

When he entered the house, Masculine was crying and immediately his heart sank. He was very protective of his sisters and wanted nothing bad to happen to them. From the time Maria had taught Mark to cook for his sisters and to make sure they were fed, Mark had never stopped looking after them in the best way he could. He wanted his sisters to feel his love, to compensate for the absence of their mother and the death of their father. He noticed that Agnes was sitting on her couch. He was surprised that Agnes wasn't comforting Masculine who was still crying.

"What is it Masculine? Are you all right?" he asked. Mark walked over to his sister and took her hand gently, "Tell me, Masculine, your brother is here; tell me what happened?" Mark looked at her sister with compassion. Masculine missed her mother and often found solace in crying as a way of easing her emotions as well as attracting attention. Masculine stopped sobbing, walked to the couch and sat next to Mark. He embraced her, and she lowered her head on Mark's lap and fell asleep. Mark turned to Agnes inquiringly, and Agnes said, "Listen! I will tell you why she is crying." Agnes explained that Masculine's friend, Lucia, had come to the house with her mother to ask Masculine to join them on a two-week vacation in Southwark. I declined to give the permission without Maria's consent. The request was at short notice since Maria is at St Columbus. So Lucia and her mother went their way without Masculine. This is why she was crying," said Agnes.

Masculine had never been away from home, and when the opportunity presented itself, she became very excited about the prospect of travelling to Southwark. She looked forward to coming back to tell everyone about her vacation. She didn't understand why Agnes refused to the request, as Lucia's mother was a good neighbour. Mark appreciated Agnes's reason for declining the offer. He lifted the sleeping Masculine from his lap and placed her in bed. When she woke up later, she had seemingly forgotten about the trip to Southwark.

Chapter 10

The ambition and the self-discovery

One weekend, Mark woke up early and assigned his sister's different house chores. He then went out to work in the garden, watering and mulching the flower beds and mowing the lawn. Agnes liked staying in bed a little longer on weekends before she took a bath and joined the grandchildren for breakfast. Mark started training himself to handle challenging work as part of his preparation for difficult times ahead. He sensed that his life was going to be difficult and he needed to learn to work hard if he was going to achieve anything significant.

Soon after breakfast, Mark took a walk to stretch his legs and headed to the park. As he walked through the neighbourhood, he admired the beautiful houses on large plots, some with swimming pools and exquisite gardens, and others with basketball and tennis courts. One such house was a magnificent double storey building on a large plot overlooking the Glenroy valley. The balcony had tinted glass windows. At the gate were a gleaming brass mailbox and a gravelled driveway led to two imposing garage doors. Also on the driveway were children's bikes and toys but no sign of the youngsters. A huge swimming pool, a tennis court and manicured green lawns must have made it the envy of neighbours.

Mark wondered whether the owner of the house was a businessman and if so, what business he was in. "This is the kind of house I want to buy for mother. How much money do I need to buy a similar house?" he asked himself. "What do I have to do to own a similar house?" Immediately he shut his eyes, and he began to envision his dream house, the plot size, the location and the facilities he liked, and then he walked away.

Mark sat in the park, contemplating the reality of his life. He came to an understanding that his family was poor and didn't even own a small house. He shared a room with his cousin Dominic. He didn't have enough space for his school books. He realised that this was the most Agnes could offer. What did he have to do when grown up to fulfil his dream of buying his mother a house? His aim was to purchase a house his family could call home. He needed someone to teach him how to realise his dream but where does a child without a father find someone like that? None of his uncles cared about him and his sisters, besides none of them seemed ambitious enough to attract his attention. They all seemed contented in the mediocrity of their lives. His mother had to work to get them food and clothes and to pay school levy. Mark was convinced by Mr Wood of the importance of education. Mark gazed wistfully into the blue sky. "When I get to high school, I want to work hard and pass. When I finish school, I want to find a job so I can help Mum support my sisters. I want my family to be happy and stay together in one house."

Mark looked at himself and despaired at the thought of his life. A few months earlier, Agnes had threatened to return the children to their uncles in Roselle. Mark and his sisters couldn't remember anything about the place, and they hadn't seen or heard anything about their uncles for many years. They feared that Agnes's heart had changed and the children thought it was their fault that Agnes was saying that. Their self-esteem dropped, and they felt unwanted and sorry for themselves. When Mark thought about his dream house, he smiled and imagined how his family would each have their rooms. His room would be upstairs, and he would come down every morning to greet his mother. From that day onwards, Mark took notice of the beautiful houses in his neighbourhood and rated each one against the house in Glenroy valley.

Agnes was standing admiring the flowers that bedecked the garden that Mark had established when the gate buzzer rang. She looked up and saw Conrad's car. She hastened to open the gate and Conrad, and his family drove in. "Oh! I wasn't expecting you," she exclaimed.

"Well, we thought we should surprise you today," replied Conrad as he clambered out the car with his children. "Seems like you are alone?"

"No, not at all! Martha and Masculine are inside the house. Come in and meet them," Agnes replied. "Dominic has gone to work and won't be back until evening, and Mark took a walk to stretch his legs a few minutes ago. He will be back soon."

Just then Mark arrived. "Welcome, Uncle!" He ran up to Conrad and embraced him. They all went inside, Agnes and Beauty moved into the kitchen to prepare food while Conrad and Mark sat in the living room in conversation. Mark told his uncle that he wanted to go to high school in Southwark when he passed

Steps in the Middle

his examinations at junior school, and he needed a place to stay. Meanwhile, Beauty had entered the room and seemed interested to overhear the discussion. Conrad hesitated for a moment and said, "I will discuss this with Beauty and Granny. Have you told Granny of your plan?"

"No, I haven't, but I will tell her now," Mark replied. He stood up, but before he could take the first step, Agnes walked into the room just in time for Mark to make the announcement. He said, "Granny, I want to go and continue my high school in Southwark. I have asked Uncle Conrad, and he said I should tell you." Mark paused. Agnes was not sure how to respond. She looked at Beauty and then at Conrad, and she said, "It's up to you and your uncle if you come to an agreement." Mark jumped up with excitement and thanked his uncle, presuming that everyone had agreed. Beauty frowned but remained quiet. Seemingly the idea of looking after another person, hardly a year after Bernard had left her care, didn't find favour with her. In truth, she was totally against the idea. She needed more time to be alone with her children and husband.

Conrad and Beauty didn't want Mark to stay with them and have to pay his school expenses. They had already had a bad experience taking in Bernard from his father, and taking in Mark would be worse because his mother wasn't employed in a well-paid job. Conrad saw the disapproval on Beauty's face, and his heart froze. Suddenly, he thought of an idea to preventing Mark from pursuing his ambition of living with him. His plan involved setting a challenging condition for Mark to achieve, thereby making it easier for him to refuse Mark's request if the condition wasn't met. He told Mark that he would only take him in if he were the best at the school. He felt sure that Mark wouldn't be able to achieve such a difficult condition. Beauty thought as much too, judging from Mark's previous academic records.

However, Mark felt happy with the idea of going to school in Southwark, even if he didn't know whether he was going to achieve the examination outcome required of him. When Conrad and his family left, Agnes said she wasn't sure if it was a good idea. "You didn't tell me about your plans of going to school in Southwark before," she remarked.

"No, I just thought about it today when I saw Uncle Conrad. I heard that there are better schools in Southwark, and if I pass my examination here, I want to go to a better school," replied Mark.

"Did you speak to Maria about it? How will you manage in such a big city?" Agnes asked. "No, I haven't talked to Mom, but I will tell her when I pass my examination. I don't know Southwark, but I will manage."

Agnes saw the determination on Mark's face. She appreciated that he was maturing faster than other boys of his age. He was responsible for keeping the house clean, the garden tidy and the lawn mown. She was relieved of the work she used to do when Maria's children first arrived. Now they washed and ironed their clothes, and Mark cooked most of the meals. But she had noticed the expression on Beauty's face and was afraid of incurring her wrath. Agnes's two other sons, Sylvester and Benedict, lived in Southwark. Although Sylvester had a bigger family than Conrad, she wasn't very comfortable with Sylvester's wife, Carol, looking after Mark. Agnes's heart was divided; she didn't want Mark to leave either. He looked after the house, and she could trust him to run her errands. Also, her health had started to decline in recent years.

Agnes's thoughts shifted to Maria, whose employment

income had improved the family's standard of living, benefitting her and the grandchildren. Maria was not only sending supplies every month but also clothes and shoes, gifts she wasn't expecting. The floral dresses she had received from Maria, in fashion at the time, fitted her perfectly. When she wore it to church, her friend Caroline spoke highly of her appearance. They had been friends for a long time, and when Caroline made a positive statement about something, it was because she meant it. On that day, Caroline invited Agnes for tea, and the two had a pleasant afternoon together. Agnes regarded the dress as one of her most prized possessions, and she wore it on important occasions to impress. Maria bought Agnes many items of clothing, more than she had occasions to wear them. Life had also become easier with Dominic now working in Patrick's business, and his income also contributed significantly to the family budget.

But not everything in the garden was rosy. Agnes's health deteriorated, and she would sometimes wake up with swollen legs, which her doctor attributed to unstable blood pressure. Occasionally, her face would be swollen, so that she would spend some days unable to see properly. Her leg joints would be painful for days, and she sought relief by massage and immersion in warm water. Agnes would recline under the tree in the middle of her front yard after breakfast every day, when the weather was favourable, listening to the radio and watching people strolling up and down the street.

Chapter

11

Teaching manners and charity at home

Maria's generosity was her way of appeasing Agnes for the burden of caring for her children. She knew from the comments she passed when Aletta came home, that Agnes didn't want to look after her kids. Agnes appreciated the clothes but was also a generous giver. She passed on some of Maria's apparel to friends and relatives in need. Agnes also gave away money and food when she was able to, thus becoming famous in the community for her generosity.

One cold and wet morning, a beggar came to Agnes's gate, shivering from the weather. Agnes went to meet the stranger and brought him inside. The man's teeth were chattering so he couldn't speak properly. She immediately ordered fire to be lit and pulled up a chair for him to take a seat next to the fire. His wet clothes started steaming because of warmth. He drank several cups of tea and devoured the hot porridge that Agnes brought him before he was able to speak. The man became stable, and he thanked Agnes profusely. He narrated events of his journey and explained that he had lost his money to robbers while travelling to another town. Agnes prepared lunch for him to eat on his way and gave him money before he departed. The beggar sang a song of gratitude and danced in the house, much to the amusement of Agnes's grandchildren. Mark, Martha and Masculine, who witnessed this drama, were initially scared when the man walked into the house. His hair was shaggy and uncombed, and his clothes were ragged and dirty. Agnes was undeterred by this, and when he left, his appearance had improved. He no longer seemed to be the same man who was on the verge of collapsing. He had regained his strength and recovered his confidence.

Whatever the misgivings of the grandchildren had been when the visitor arrived, they were in awe of Agnes's kindness and open-heartedness. Agnes had previously shown herself to be a generous person mostly towards women and that day, she exhibited another dimension of her character, never to look down on anyone in need.

A few weeks later, Marks examinations results were out. To the astonishment of his classmates and teachers not to mention his family, he came out top in the junior examination. The headmaster wanted him to enrol at Casterbridge High School, but Mark requested instead for a recommendation letter so that he could enrol in Southwark. Agnes knew exactly what that meant. Her fears were about to be realised. How could she stop Mark now after coming on top of his class? Agnes acquiescently agreed to let Mark have his way. Mark had never been to Southwark, and so Agnes found someone to help him with directions. He hardly slept on the night before his trip. Mark rose early and prepared to depart. Agnes walked him to the gate and, as was her custom with every child leaving, she gave him some words of wisdom.

"You are going to join a new family, where nobody knows you well. Be good to everyone and especially to the children of Conrad and Beauty. You are going to Southwark to attain your goals. Don't quit and don't return home empty-handed. In any endeavour, patience and persistence are hallmarks of success. Always do what you are assigned to with graciousness and with a smile. A smile never costs you anything. Don't give anyone cause to send you back to Casterbridge before you finish school. Don't complain, don't be disobedient and don't be disrespectful."

Agnes was a persuasive counsellor, and her sons and neighbours often sought her advice. Mark was already expecting her to say something before he left and she didn't disappoint him. He was familiar with the content of her lectures, and the lectures were part of the ritual of departure. Finally, when Agnes concluded by giving Mark, a hug and Mark stepped away with a happy smile. Agnes remained standing as Marked strolled away, she couldn't believe the sight of Mark taking a trip by himself for the first time. Mark was also excited by the prospect of travelling to Southwark for the first time. From that point on, he knew he was responsible for his life. He was anxious but at the same time confident that he could achieve his ambition. He hoped that he could live happily with Conrad's family.

With his bag in one hand and scribbled directions in his pocket, Mark left Agnes's gate, walked to the bus stop and boarded the coach to Southwark. It was an exciting ride as he pushed aside worries of being lost in a big city, of being robbed of his bag and his money being stolen. The money that Agnes had given him was sufficient to get him to Southwark, and she had a packed lunch box that morning.

Steps in the Middle

When the coach left Casterbridge and sped down the highway towards Southwark, it passed through other towns and villages that were unknown to Mark. In one large town, the residential streets were deserted of pedestrians; the city dwellers appeared to drive more than walk. The houses were impressive. There was one double-storey house built on what seemed like ten hectares of land, its garage accommodating three cars and outside was another carport which could fit another three cars. Behind the house was a paddock where several horses were grazing unperturbed by cars and buses moving up and down the road. Large square bales of hay filled the ban a short walk from the house. Everything in the neighbourhood looked serene and calm. It was indeed a new level of beauty that he saw for the first time.

As the journey progressed, town life outside the coach window was replaced by farm life. Mark's gaze took in vast tracts of land with crops and livestock. Tractors drawing various implements were busy in the fields. Further down the farm, his eye came to the farmer's house and nearby, was a workshop and various other farm implements. "What does it take to become a farmer?" he thought. "Do all these cattle belong to one person? I would love to live on a farm, keeping rearing livestock. I hope I will be able to do that one day." Mark was confronted by a new level of wealth and success that he had not seen before in Casterbridge. He wondered why some people were poor, and could not afford a meal while others had plenty of wealth. He wondered why some people lived in high-rise building while others owned vast tracks of land. To none of these questions did he find answers.

After more than an hour, the coach entered Southwark, and he was greeted with the glitter and glamour of a new city. Southwark bustled with people hurrying up and down. The streets were jammed with cars. Tall buildings almost blocked out the sun. The driver brought the coach to a complete halt at the terminus, took his microphone and thanked the passengers and bid them farewell. The coach was on time, and everyone has thanked him as they stepped out. As the people disembarked, he signalled to Mark. "You said you are going to Claremont, is that right?" he asked. "Yes, sir," replied Mark. The driver directed him to a bus stop on the other side of the station. Mark thanked him and hoisted his bag onto his back and hurried in the direction indicated. Southwark had more people than he ever imagined and he would have to adapt to a new pace of life.

In due course, Mark arrived in Claremont, a residential suburb clearly less affluent that the other suburbs on the way. The houses were smaller, but the people seemed friendly and relaxed, and that put him at ease. Conrad's house was not easy to find, and with his bag on his back, Mark combed the streets of Claremont looking for it. Soon he realised that he had disembarked two stops past Conrad's house. His bag was heavy, and he was sweating profusely when, after nearly an hour of fear and panic, he found Conrad's house. He had passed it twice walking on the other side of the street. When he arrived Beauty was in her bedroom, and one of her children opened the door for Mark. He lowered his bag from his back and in the process dragged his shirt from his trousers. His shoes were dusty, leaving tracks on the floor tiles. Mark hurriedly tucked in his shirt before looking around. The house was well kept, the furniture polished and shiny, and the fresh scent in the house greeted him. Beauty's first-born son, Chester, ran into his mother's bedroom and after a long while, Beauty emerged, looking sternly at Mark who was seated on the couch.

"Welcome, Mark." Her words were hardly in keeping with the

expression on her face. Mark felt nervous at her reception. He greeted her politely and told her that he had passed his examinations and that was why he had come to stay with them, as per their previous promise. Beauty held her tongue and looked displeased. Mark extended his hand, with his certificate in hand, to give proof to Beauty. On the other hand, Beauty declined to take it. Mark withdrew his hand and placed the certificate back in his bag. He remained silent. Beauty turned round abruptly went to her bedroom. Mark remained seated on the couch. He figured out that she was shocked either because he had come out top in his class or that he was coming to live with her family. Beauty stood up without a word and disappeared into her bedroom.

A while later Beauty emerged from her bedroom again and sat on the couch next to Mark. She was a little more composed than before. Mark, who was feeling hungry while waiting for Beauty, took out his pre-packed lunch prepared by Agnes and began eating. "How did you find this place?" Beauty asked. Mark described everything that had happened from when he got the address to how he connected to Claremont.

"So have you come to stay with us now? Does your mother know? How many years are you going to be living with us?" Beauty asked. She forced a smile, barely showing her teeth out and there was sweat on her nose.

"Yes," replied Mark. "I asked uncle if I could stay with you until I finished my high school and he agreed. I sent my mother a letter, and I think she has received it by now, she is possibly aware." Mark paused.

"You want to stay with us for six years! That's a damn long time." Beauty exclaimed.

Mark realised that she was really unhappy about his presence in her house. "If uncle allows me to stay until I finish my school, that will take six years," Mark replied. She didn't like Mark's response, feeling that Mark's stay didn't only depend on Conrad's word but on how she felt too. Beauty looked at Mark's bag on the floor; it was indeed evident that Mark had come to stay with her family. Beauty picked up Mark's bag and walked into another room in the house. She stayed there for a while, pushing and pulling things about noisily as if she was re-arranging furniture there.

After a while Beauty emerged from the room and called Mark. "This will be your room. I have put your bag here, and this will be your bed." The room was small with just enough space for a single bed but no other furniture. There was nowhere to hang his clothes, and so Mark's clothes remained in his bag, which she had suspended against the wall. The only place to sit was on the bed. Two little windows high up the wall were not accessible without the aid of a ladder. The room had previously been used as a store room, and Beauty had chosen it for Mark so that she wouldn't disrupt the family's sleeping arrangements. Beauty's children were much younger than Mark, and her son Chester had just started junior school that year. Mark helped Beauty tidy the room, and from his bag, he pulled sheets and make the bed. When they were finished, Mark sat alone in the room, and he began to think through his next steps. With the door closed, the room immediately became stuffy, and Mark stepped on the bed to reach the windows before he flung them open. He wasn't used to sleeping alone as he had always shared a room with his cousin Dominic. That night he slept fitfully.

For four days, Conrad didn't return home from work early enough to meet Mark before he retired to bed. It wasn't until Friday morning that Conrad knocked on Mark's door early in the morning to greet him before leaving without much conversation. Mark was surprised at his uncles' behaviour which was unlike him. Previous when Conrad had visited Casterbridge, he had always appeared happy and jovial, and on that morning Conrad's face totally lacked emotion. Mark expected him to request him for his certificate and congratulate him for his examination success, but as he walked out of his room, shutting the door behind him, he knew he wasn't interested. He had hope that Conrad would be shocked with his examination success, but his mind seemed far away from the present. Conrad appeared to have come to meet him, that morning, to fulfil a formality and ritual of greeting.

Mark observed that Beauty was afraid of Conrad and when he came back from work, the couple didn't talk freely or laugh together. Although Conrad occasionally played with his daughter, Olivia, the rest of the children were afraid of him. Every time the children heard Conrad's car driving into the garage, they would disappear quietly indoors and pretend to be studying their books. They would emerge during meal times and quickly disappear into their rooms like squirrels running away from a predator. Whenever it was meal time, all the children would emerge from their rooms and proceed to the table, partook their meals, cleaned up and immediately disappeared back to their rooms. The children's behaviour contrasted sharply with their midday behaviour when Conrad would be away.

Every day, they repeated this behaviour until they were so good at it, to the extent that they didn't need to think about it. They established silent codes to alert each other and communicate the arrival of their father; information was passed from the eldest to the youngest with remarkable efficiency. Mark, too, became scared of Conrad such that whenever he came back from work, his heart would pound in fear. Mark found this situation very disturbing. This wasn't the same uncle he spoke to confidently when Conrad last visited Casterbridge. His presence terrified his family.

When Mark first walked into Conrad's house, he was filled with admiration. "They have a good life; I wish he were my father. What else would I want," he thought. It was a large house compared to many others in the neighbourhood, overlooking the main road into Claremont. The small garden in front was neatly laid out with roses and other flowers that not only attracted bees but also the attention of people walking past. They would stop to admire the flowers and take photographs of the garden. Inside the house, the tiled kitchen was well designed and fitted with expensive accessories. A large refrigerator stood on one side and a matching stove on the other. Many other gadgets in the kitchen must have made cooking a pleasure; quite different from Agnes's kitchen in Casterbridge.

Inside; the house was painted white, and the couches in the living room were large and comfortable. Two portraits hung from each side of the fireplace. A large glass door provided access to the spacious balcony with modern outdoor furniture where one could enjoy the sun and observe the goings-on in Claremont. Curtains could be drawn across the windows to shield the room from direct sunlight when needed. An elaborate chandelier hung from the ceiling.

Mark woke up early next morning with Agnes's word fresh in his mind, "If you want to succeed you have to focus on your goal." He told himself, "Don't be deceived by the beauty that you see in this house, it is not yours. You are not part of this family. Wake up! Go and enrol yourself now!" Mark reached for his wristwatch; the time was just after midnight. He had only slept for a few hours. He fell back into a fitful sleep, waking several times before morning. His goal of registering at school in Southwark was all important, and nothing would stop him. He didn't know the whereabouts of the closest school, and after Beauty's reaction to him the previous day he was aware that she would not be interested in his school matters. He would have to make his education a personal thing.

Mark missed his mother. He hadn't seen her for months. "I want to tell her my plans; I know she would listen." Tears ran down his cheeks. The excitement of coming to Southwark quickly faded away. He felt lonely; there was no one to share his hopes and ambitions. He appreciated that she had to work to pay the school levy for him and his sisters. He told himself, "You've got to be a man now, and men don't cry. So, come on! Get on with what you came to do here and stop crying for her. This is not the time for that! You are the first-born and the only boy child of your mother. She is looking to you, to acquire a better education than she did. You are already standing on her shoulders; what else do you want? Here is your chance to do better and help her.

Keep moving forward; and if you do, you will be her only consolation for what she didn't achieve. Focus on the chance at hand! You will never know how good you are until you try. Where is your faith? You said you are Christian. You told your sisters you are their big brother and you fought other boys to protect them, now you are crying when no one is fighting with you. Cowards shed tears; are you one? Are you giving up the fight before you even begin or did you think it was going to be easy? Do you want to quit? Your mother didn't quit looking after you. If you quit now, you'll always be quitting on your family and everything. You are the only person they are looking up to. You will have disowned her and what good is a son, if he disowns his family. You and your family live in other people's homes. You said you wanted to buy a big house and you walked around viewing houses as if you wanted to buy.

Didn't you know that it would cost you something? Did you not know that he, who desires to reach the mountain top, has to wrestle with the climb before he conquers the summit? You have no father, so stop looking for one! You have to learn to be a father to your sisters and start being a good example. What kind of man do you want to become? Agnes told you that your dad was a hard worker. Why can't you be like him?" The voice inside him tormented him every moment.

Mark's bag was still suspended on a wall nail, the only wall nail in the room where Beauty had placed it the previous day. He grabbed it and took out fresh clothes. His dusty shoes lay next to his bed. The windows were still closed, and room was hot and stuffy. He climbed on his bed, reached for the window and flung it open. Studying his map, he figured out the location of all the closest schools. He carefully prepared his documents including his certificate and was ready to leave the house. Beauty and family were still in bed. As Mark walked out of his room, Beauty appeared. "Good morning, Mark, did you sleep well?" She asked with a radiating smile.

"Good morning Beauty, I am ready to leave for schools now," Mark replied.

Beauty said, "I want to help you find the best school around since you have excellent results. Can I see your certificate?" Beauty studied Mark's certificate as if she had doubts about his claims of passing, yet the previous day she wasn't interested in looking at it. Beauty described the various schools in Claremont, some of which Mark had already listed. He was ready to go out when Beauty suggested that he could prepare breakfast for himself before leaving. Mark declined, saying he wanted to enrol first. She was surprised at his decision, and for the first time she felt compassion for him; she could see how determined he was about getting his education. She noticed that his clothes, although neat, were somewhat tatty. His shirt had been washed so many times, it was diaphanous.

Mark's eyes were glowing with enthusiasm and confidence. He looked like he had just won an Olympic gold medal. His attitude was in sharp contrast to that of her son, Chester, who disliked school with a passion. Every school day for Chester was a pain, he would whine about going to school. Sometimes, Chester pretended to be ill to avoid going to school. Often he would stay in bed all morning pretending to be sick, and his illness would seem to end immediately after taking breakfast. This practice suddenly stopped when Beauty hinted that was going to alert Conrad about his illness. Chester left for school immediately without any further arguments. Beauty thought Mark's enthusiasm for education would be a good example to Chester. She thought Mark would help Chester with his school work rather than her.

Mark left the house and hurried down the street. It was still early when he arrived at Glen View High School, and he sat outside until staff arrived. The school was relatively new and looked well-endowed with facilities. Mark regarded it with admiration. When the teaching staff began to arrive, he noticed that most drove their cars and a few took a ride with colleagues. Mark compared the cars and soon realised that he didn't know much about cars. He tried to speculate who the headmaster was by looking at the cars arriving in the car park. Then suddenly a small red car came. "This must be the headmaster's car," he thought. The driver seemed to crouch down in his seat to avoid bumping his head on the roof. He rolled down the window and peered out to check that he had parked the car correctly. This must have given much-needed relief to his bent neck.

After switching off the engine, a tall, slender man clambered out. He must have practised getting in and out of his car because of his height. "Perhaps that where the fun is of buying such a small car," thought Mark. His arms were longer than the space available as he sat in the driver's seat. As soon as the driver was out, he stretched his arms and legs as if he desperately needed it. He wiped his sweaty face with a handkerchief before lighting a cigarette. "Could it be that he is calming his nerves," Mark thought, "But why would such a tall man buy such a small, stylish car? Didn't he test drive it to see if he could fit into it comfortably?" Mark asked himself. The man ground out his cigarette without paying attention to Mark and after while he strode past Mark towards the building.

To the west of the school offices were two student entrances into the campus. Many students were dropped by their parents in smart cars. Some students appeared to come from very affluent families judging by the cars their parents drove. Some drove themselves, and yet others walked from nearby residences. Mark observed how the students conversed with one another and how they were dressed. He felt somewhat despondent. He was zealous to start school immediately, yet he was uncertain about his mother's ability to pay school levies and buy school uniforms. None of the students appeared to come from low-income families, and Mark queried whether his record, even if excellent, would be sufficient reason for successful enrolment. What if he was offered a vacancy and didn't have the money to pay the school levy? He didn't even know how much the school levy was. He was also worried about his clothing which did not match that of the students there.

"If I tell Mom that I need new clothes first, she may not have enough money for school levies as well. I would be humiliated coming to school with only the clothes that I have," he thought. "Perhaps I should go to another school where the parents aren't that wealthy."

Then he remembered Agnes's words about focusing on his goals. "Perhaps, I shouldn't worry about clothes at this stage. Let me wait till I get a vacancy and then I can share with mum the list of requirements. Hopefully, she will be able to send me what she can afford. My sisters also want books, so I shouldn't put too much pressure on Mum," Mark thought. When I grow up, I will support my mother and take over all the financial demands from her. Mr Wood told me that if I keep working hard, I will get what I want," Mark said to himself.

While Mark was still pondering these thoughts, the front office door was flung open, and out came a man dressed in a suit. "Good morning, all you prospective students," he shouted. There was a sudden silence, and the sound of the clock ticking on the wall could be heard. Mark had been waiting for more than an hour at the front door, and the queue had grown long by the time the office door opened. Most other students in the queue had their parents standing next to them. "Was it a requirement to bring parents? Would Beauty have agreed to come with me to the school? I don't think so. If they refuse to enrol me without my parents, I will try another school before asking Beauty," Mark resolved.

"Today, we are enrolling the students who passed with

distinctions," the teacher called out. "If you scored maximum points, please come to the front." Mark rushed to the front hoping to avoid being crowded by other achievers, but there were only two others.

"Well done, you three. Welcome to Glen View High School. Complete these forms and when you are finished bring them along with your certificates." shouted the Teacher. Mark wasted no time in completing the forms and in a few minutes was standing before the teacher's desk. The teacher looked at Mark's certificates, smiled and shook his hand before processing his enrolment. Mark was grateful that his good results were giving him access to this school. His self-esteem grew, and his confidence was bolstered for a moment. He felt good about himself and that he could reach his ambitions at Glen View High School.

"You are now enrolled," the teacher said. "Take this form to pay the school levy. It has your reference number. You will be given a document to sign which sets out the rules of the school, and you'll get a copy for yourself. Your classes commence next week on Monday. The list of all stationery requirements and textbooks is included in the pack that you received. Read the documents carefully and if you have any questions come back and ask me," he concluded.

To Mark's relief, the school levy looked reasonable. He was thrilled that his goal of passing junior school examinations with distinctions and leaving Casterbridge to attend school in Southwark had now been achieved. He felt a sense of accomplishment as he collected his enrollment confirmation and walked triumphantly from the school office. Mark hurried off to break the news to Beauty.

When he arrived, Beauty seemed in no mode to talk. She

didn't even ask him about enrolment. Mark was hungry and expected to be offered breakfast like he had been that morning, but this wasn't forthcoming. He went to his room, shut the door and sat quietly on his bed. He was disturbed by Beauty's attitude and was wondering why one moment she was happy and another very moody. That morning, Beauty looked happy when he left home, but by midday, things had changed. He stayed in his room until late afternoon. Chester and his sisters were playing outside and weren't worried about, besides they were still young. As every minute passed, his stomach began aching with hunger. He stood up and offered Beauty help with her chores. He found Beauty sitting in the lounge. "Do you want me to assist you with anything?" he asked. Beauty remained silent as if she didn't hear the question. Mark repeated his offer. "No, I don't need anything. Go to your room and rest," she replied looking away.

Mark went back to his room and shut the door behind him again. The desire to share his news with someone was tormenting him, not to mention the hunger. Mark felt he was forcing himself on a family that didn't want him. Was he selfish to expect these people to celebrate his success? Clearly, Beauty didn't like him. Was it worth coming to Southwark after all? Why was it necessary to beg for accommodation? Mark pondered over many questions, but he couldn't get easy answers.

Mark knew for certain that he had come to Southwark to complete his education. He needed to do so to achieve his dream of becoming successful. He would have to make peace with Beauty and her family; failing which he would be sent back to Casterbridge before completing school. Mark resolved to do anything Beauty demanded, without complaining or questioning. He would only eat the food given to him and only do as asked and he knew his life with Beauty's family would be hard and painful.

"Who can I talk to, and who can help me? I wish Mr Wood were nearby, I would have gone to his house and told him everything, and maybe he would have helped me. If I quit because of pain and hunger, I will never get another chance. Agnes said 'winners never quit'. I thought that people who live in beautiful houses could never be unhappy. A man without a house wishes if only he had a beautiful house he'd be happy. For a fact, now I have seen that happiness doesn't come from the things one possesses, but rather one's emotional state. Maybe I am paying the price for transforming my life, from being an impoverished rural boy to someone great. Is this price worth paying? How else can I explain why I have to go through this trying time? I can't see any other option at the moment.

I am the one who needs the knowledge and therefore I have to pay the equivalent price of getting it. But does everyone pay the price for what they want in life or does it applies only to fatherless boys? If life is fair, which I believe it is, everyone will have to pay the price for whatever they ask life to give them. If life is fair, it will give me back the equivalent of what I am going to pay for, nothing less or more. If everyone pays in life, then this is my turn to pay." Marked continued musing on the challenges he was facing. After a moment, Mark took pen and paper from his bag, and he wrote a letter to his mother, informing her about the list of requirements at his new school. He stood up and walked to the Post Office to send the letter.

After a week of living with Beauty and Conrad, Mark was now more familiar with the dysfunction in his uncle's family. Beauty opened up to him and explained that infidelity was causing the tension between her and Conrad. Conrad often stayed out all

Steps in the Middle

night without giving her any explanation. His marriage to Beauty was a farce, devoid of any meaningful communication. The last time the two tried to discuss the matter, Conrad burst with anger and suddenly became verbally abusive, after which they never spoke to each other for weeks. Whenever there was a guest, he would quickly change his mood to give a false impression that all was well. As soon as the guest leaves, Conrad would immediately resume his mood. Whenever Conrad was home, his silent treatment of Beauty was more painful than anything she had ever experienced. She yearned for him to speak and laugh like they did when they first got married. Their marriage was already dead; they just hadn't made it official yet. It was the children that kept Beauty and Conrad under the same roof. They were sharing the same room for the sack of convenience. Conrad was also still holding onto the marriage for the sake of the symbolism that marriage offered, yet in reality, his heart was no longer with her. For some reason, neither of them wanted to be the first to quit.

On the other hand, some women, unaware of Beauty's marriage nightmares envied her and wished they were married to Conrad. The viewed him through the lenses of his possessions, and their cravings for material support. Beauty despised Conrad's wealth. She attributed it to the emptiness of their marriage. On the other hand, her extended family treated her as royalty and people jostled amongst each other to get closer to her because of her husband's fame. Everyone wanted to be closer to Beauty because of the fame her family enjoyed, while Beauty remained humble, and firmly focused on her career as a fulltime housewife. She often thought of leaving him, but the prospect of leaving her children behind always stood in her way. If that were to happen, Conrad would quickly find another mate.

Beauty dreaded the idea of her children being raised by a stepmother. She kept hoping desperately that Conrad would come to his sense and realise his error. Frequently she would dream of Conrad apologising to her for his errors but that never actually came true. When this didn't happen, Beauty's four children became her abiding source of pride and comfort.

When Beauty confided with Mark, he became aware that his presence in their house was not the main reason for Beauty's unhappiness. Mark became to see a different Beauty he hadn't seen when he first arrived, he saw Beauty like a little girl trying hard to get the attention from her mother, but continuously ignored. After failing to get the attention of Conrad, she needed someone to whom she could empty her heart and share her frustrations with. The only available person to hear her was Mark. Within a few conversations, Mark couldn't bear to listen to some of the details she spoke about. On the other hand, Beauty enjoyed his attention even though he only offered sympathy and a hearing ear. For many months, Beauty would wait for Mark to get back from school so that she could share with him her frustrations of the day.

Mark wondered why his uncle neglected his family. Conrad wore smart clothes, was a famous and successful businessman in Casterbridge and yet his success in business was not replicated at home. Conrad did not want Beauty to be involved in his business or get to know how much money he was earning. He kept his financial affairs under lock and key and would get paranoid if Beauty moved his papers an inch. He made it clear to her that his papers were out of bounds to her. Conrad loved to be in control of everything concerning his family. He preferred shopping for grocery alone, bringing everything on his way back from work.

Beauty was allowed to buy clothing in one store where Conrad had opened an account and would come later to the shop to pay the bill. She couldn't leave the house for any reason without him knowing where she was going. For whatever reason, Conrad felt insecure when Beauty was away from the house or engaged in a conversation with a man. He knew his wife was faithful and he thought that allowing her to be away from home, exposed her to new opportunities for an alternative lifestyle without him.

Conrad controlled Beauty's life, carefully monitoring every step she took and every word she uttered, who she spoke to and where. Nothing could be done without his knowledge and approval. Beauty and the children knew that any mistakes they made would result in a barrage of rude words from him. Although he did not physically discipline his children, the fear he instilled in them from a young age, was chilling. His children would freeze when he spoke, and they would run when sent anywhere. Conrad's big eyes were enough to scare the wits out of the children, who were not accustomed to any other way their father behaved. They would never think of upsetting their father willingly. Beauty loved to be active, she yearned for helping out in Conrad's business, but Conrad couldn't stand coming in the limelight of his business. Ultimately, he didn't want Beauty to end up getting to know his financial affairs.

Conrad didn't want Beauty to acquire anything that would give her power over him or to be independent of him. He made sure she relied on him for income, food, affection and everything except her breath. Conrad manipulated Beauty's life, turning and twisting it whenever he pleased. This titillated his ego and made him feel like a real man, the sole, supreme and unchallenged provider of his family. He enjoyed fraying her emotions, and those actions gave him the stimulus that he needed to feel like a man.

Chapter

12

Standing up for yourself when no one is available

Three weeks after Mark resumed classes at Glen View High School; his school levy was yet to be paid. His excellent grades from junior school had earned him a vacancy, but his inability to pay school levy on time was beginning to bother the school administration. The headmaster summoned him from class one morning. Mark followed the headmaster to his office; his legs were trembling in fear because he didn't why had was being called apart from his unpaid levy. "Does he want to withdrawal my enrolment", he thought. Seating behind the desk, the headmaster, Mr John Donaldson, a Scotsman with a heavy accent, opened the file on his desk and frowned. "I notice you haven't yet paid school levy and it is now more than three weeks after you started classes. Didn't you receive the enrolment pack containing enrollment requirement and the payment forms? When are you going to pay?" he demanded with a bumming voice.

He raised his eyes from the file and looked straight into Mark's eyes. Mark lifted his head with guilt and shame, and calmly replied, "Yes, I received the enrolment pack, and I haven't paid because my mother hasn't sent the money." Looking puzzled the headmaster, replied, "Where is your mom? Can you give me her telephone number so that I can call her right away or else can you bring her to my office before the end of the day?" Mr Donaldson appeared agitated.

"I don't live with my parents, sir. I live with my uncle and his family. My mother works at an orphanage at St Columbus. I wrote to her immediately after my enrollment. I know she will pay the school levy as soon as she receives my letter. She has never failed to pay my school levy ever since I started school. Please allow her more time to pay," Mark beseeched. Mr Donaldson looked at Mark with searching eyes. He was considering whether he could trust Mark's mother whom he had never seen, but the boy's passionate plea struck a chord. In his more than five-year tenure at Glen View High School, he had never encountered a student defending their parent's delay in paying school levy with such fervour.

For a moment, he was tempted to send Mark aware and cancel his enrollment, but something on Mark tempted him to hold back his impatience. Mark knew the power of the Headmaster to terminate his registration, and his heart was stirred to defend his delay in paying school levy. He held his head high and sat straight in his chair, looked at the Headmaster in front of him. His eyes told a story which convinced Mr Donaldson to keep him in school a little longer.

"Listen, Mark, I will give you until the end of the month to sort out your financial affairs, and if you fail to pay, I will have to cancel your registration. The school cannot keep a student who can't meet the entire enrollment requirements." Mr Donaldson spoke firmly, closing Mark's file. Mark hastened back to class, thinking, "Why do I have to fight for everything that I need. Other students have their school levies paid by their parents without delay. Is it because I am an orphan and that my father is no longer alive? My mother is overwhelmed with work; she can't be in two places at once," he mused.

Mark knew that Conrad and Beauty weren't interested in his education. They were not willing to assist him with any financial and material needs apart from accommodation and food, as per their previous conversation. They were ready to support him during the semester, but during school vacations, he would have to go back to Casterbridge.

Then, in answer to his prayers, Maria arrived, bringing with her money for Mark's school levy, as well as toiletries and bed linen. She had taken a few days off and headed straight for Southwark. Maria brought not only money for the school levy but also second-hand clothes that she had bought at the fundraising event while at St Columbus. Mark was happy to receive this apparel, although some garments were too small because Mark had grown taller. Charity events at St Columbus were held when clothes donated from different parts of the country had accumulated sufficiently to warrant another sale. Second-hand clothes were important for Maria as she was not able to afford new clothes for the children, and she always chose carefully because clothes bought at fundraising events could not be returned. Mark had no problem with the clothes his mother brought him, although some school children laughed as he walked past. "Young man, did you inherit those clothes from your grandfather?" they mocked. Mark was embarrassed at first, but he was also relieved to have more than

Steps in the Middle

one set of clothes to wear. He also appreciated the efforts of his mother to support him and his sisters.

It took Mark a little longer than most children of his age to make close friends because, apart from his casual attire, he was seen by some as being too smart. "He is too serious, that boy. What can you talk to him about? He won't find anything funny" they said. This didn't bother Mark; as he had learnt to be isolated since he was in Casterbridge.

Mark did not have much time with Maria as she left Beauty's house after only an hour, hoping to reach Casterbridge before sunset. Before she left, she had a candid talk with Mark. "You know that I am a single parent, so don't compare yourself with Beauty's children or those of her neighbours. Their fathers are alive, and their parents have sufficient money to support them. You have to be satisfied with what I can bring for you. I will always do what I can.

Secondly, you came to Southwark for your education and nothing else. Beauty is doing a favour by giving you accommodation, so don't give her cause to send you back to Casterbridge before you finish high school. I don't want to hear any stories of misbehaviour. Be obedient and respectful; don't fight with her children.

Watch your words; take care of what comes out of your mouth. The mouth is like a wildfire; it can burn anything in its path, and once you light a fire, it is hard to extinguish it. If you don't have anything good to say keep quiet, and save your breath to cool your porridge. Be content with what Beauty serves on the table to eat, and be appreciative. People love a friendly person. Learn to smile and live with gladness. Make sure no one smells your bad moods. If it smells, it affects other people and their perception of you. Above all, work hard on your education.

Wake up every day, with the expectation of doing your best, in whatever you are studying at school. Don't spend too much time with friends whose destination is not the same as yours. Many people are wondering aimlessly in life, and they often want other people to join them, on their journey to the land of 'nowhere'. You, however, keep your focus before you face every day. Nothing is better than having clarity of where you are in life and vision of tomorrow. You begged Conrad to allow you to live with his family while furthering your education, so don't give him any reason to send you back to Casterbridge," Maria concluded talking, looking at Mark in his eyes. She took her hand and put it on Mark's head as if she was praying for him and then she departed. Mark had heard similar lectures many times before; he could recite Maria's words verbatim.

Her words sunk deep into his heart. "What else could I do to remain focused on my goals of getting a good education?" he thought. Mark knew that he didn't have many friends to divert his attention. He resolved to make sure that his uncle's family wouldn't misinterpret his quiet demeanour as moodiness. "My mother said I should smile every morning. Maybe this will make people around me feel happier sharing accommodation with me, and may even make them love me in return. I never thought that my mood affects other people." Mark resolved to smile whenever he spoke to Beauty and Conrad, even faking a pleasant outlook when in fact he wasn't happy.

When Mark came back from school, he greeted Conrad with a smile. Conrad continued reading his newspaper without taking his eyes off the paper. Mark walked past despondently. He felt like he didn't exist or was just nothing. "Why does he ignore me?" Then he said to himself, "You have nowhere else to stay so put up with it. When you grow up, you will buy your big house. You and everyone who stays there will be most welcome. For now, you have no control over what happens in Conrad's house. Get over it and keep moving!" The voice inside him has tormented him; Mark wanted to impress Conrad and Beauty, and again their approval. He didn't want them to think that he wasn't a good person to live with their family. He hoped one day they would perceive his heartfelt appreciation for what they had done for him. He knew he had nothing to give them in return for what they were doing for him, and so for many months that followed, he sought to repay them back by keeping a good attitude.

Mark spent many hours studying, determined to achieve a good performance at school. When he wasn't assisting Beauty with house chores, he would be reading. The fact that he didn't have many friends meant that he had more time to read. He remembered Maria's counsel that he shouldn't compare himself to other children whose parents were both alive. He acknowledged that Beauty and Conrad didn't have an obligation to look after him. They had neither bothered to help him find a school nor help him with the enrolment process. Judging by the room he had allocated, Beauty's directive on what to touch and what not, it became apparent that he was nothing more than a guest; he was lodging with them and not living with them. His days with Beauty's family were limited.

Further, he realised that people didn't care about orphans as much as they purported to. Those who professed to care only did so when it was convenient. Some helped orphans only to make a statement about themselves, to blow their trumpets. The helpers of this nature prided themselves with the approval their goodwill gestures brought them. "I wish fathers and mothers of young children would not die prematurely. It leaves the children in such a vulnerable condition. It's not the same for children whose parents are separated; they can travel from one parent to another." Mark felt miserable as he walked into his room and tears ran down his cheeks, but suddenly he cheered up with the knowledge that Maria had left an envelope with money sufficient to pay his school levy and stationery. She had added an extra amount for him to buy his other things.

CHAPTER
13

Life principles, a dysfunctional home and keeping the focus

Richard Middleton was a well-respected senior teacher at the school. For many years, he had tried to inculcate in students a value based life based on life principles which he believed were true. He emphasised the need for students to have personal principles to guide them in life, to help them make a decision in whatever situation they would encounter in life. Like any lecture given to school children, some listened, and some wouldn't listen. In giving his speech, he likened personal principles to a moral compass which would direct them in matters of education, social life, and just about everything else.

His favourite illustration involved a student who didn't smoke but could easily be influenced by his friends to start smoking because he held no position of his own. "Without personal principles," he said, "you will not be able to direct your life. No one should to tell you to stop making noise in class or focus on your school work; your principles should dictate your course of action. No one should have to supervise you to complete your assignment when you get home; your principles should be your guide. Every evening, before you sleep, check that you have carried out the most important tasks of the day. Prepare your next day's plan, listing everything in writing which will help you to remember. Remember, being busy doing things on your list doesn't mean you are effective. Focus first on the things that have the most impact in reaching your most important goals."

Mark remembered a similar lecture the previous year from Mr Wood, back in Casterbridge. He had told him about the importance of planning. While Mr Middleton was speaking, some students around him were yawning, and others couldn't wait to leave the school hall. Most of the students in the senior grades were familiar with his lectures; they had heard it many times past. Some listened attentively to Mr Middleton out of respect for his position while others listened to him because it was the right thing to do. Mark wanted to know how he could learn more about personal principles. He was excited to be part of the lecture, although he felt the presentation was not well received by the rest of the students.

Mr Middleton was strict and particularly intolerant of misbehaviour. He was regarded as a man of his word and wisdom, but most students were afraid of being suspended for indiscipline. One day, Mr Middleton stopped in the middle of his lecture; his eyes remained fixed on the back of the school hall. He was looking at a schoolgirl who was talking and making jokes, distracting the attention of other students. Mr Middleton left the podium silently, and with his eye firmly fixed on the girl, walked to her chair. He led her from the back of the school hall to the front and stood her next to the podium. He continued with his lecture for more than thirty minutes while the girl stood to face the assembly. She shivered and sweated, and to avoid the shame of looking at the class; she turned her back against Mr Middleton.

Immediately Mr Middleton said to her, "Stand facing the assembly!"

She did so but looked down with her hands in her pockets, then behind her back and then finally by her side. There was laughter from the back of the hall, and she started crying. At the end of the lecture, Mr Middleton escorted the girl to the Headmaster's office.

When Mr Middleton dismissed the students and left the hall, Mark followed and caught up with him before he entered the Headmaster's office. "Excuse me, sir," he said breathlessly. "I have a question about your lecture regarding personal principles."

Mr Middleton looked at Mark sternly. Students had to have a steady nerve to approach him with a question. His face was heavily bearded yet neatly trimmed. His bushy eyebrows exacerbated his fierce look, and deep wrinkles ran across his face. He had broad shoulders and muscular hands. He rarely smiled, and when he did, not many people would understand why. "Come and see me after I am done with the Headmaster," he thundered. The girl was still walking in front of him, and they both entered the headmaster's office. Mark went back to class, sat down and began writing down notes following Mr Middleton's lecture. It was during a break, and not many students were in the room.

Two boys were discussing the recent Manchester United versus Liverpool soccer match. He raised his head and recognised two of his classmates, Chance and Phineas. "Hey, Mark, how is it going?" asked Chance. "Did you watch the match?"

"No, I didn't. When was it?" asked Marked, packing his books.

"Last Sunday afternoon, at three o'clock. It was at the Old Trafford," replied Chance enthusiastically. He and Phineas pulled out chairs and sat around Mark. "I hear you are good in accounting, according to the teacher's comment in class yesterday," Chance continued.

"Well, I do my best. I also noted that the teacher said you got the highest marks in mathematics. Will you help me with maths when I have a problem?" Mark replied.

"Yes, I am certainly willing to help, if you need anything," replied Chance. "Yesterday I saw you walking past our house. I tried calling you, but you were walking too fast. I saw you opening the gate at the house further down the street. Is that where you stay?" Chance enquired.

Mark reasoned that Chance and Phineas were neighbours, and their respective houses were quite close to Beauty's house. Over the weekends, Chance and Phineas often watched sport on television together. Mark wasn't such an avid follower of soccer, but the following week he reluctantly accepted Chance's offer to watch a match with him, and Phineas was also there. Phineas was very reserved and modest. He was shorter than Chance and slender. He kept his hair neat and wore smart clothes to school every day, and he made sure that his shoes were always well-polished before leaving the house. He had a school bag for each day, and the quality of his clothing reflected the affluence of his parents. He had everything that boys of his age craved for, from toys to all the books he needed for his studies. However, he struggled with every subject in class. He lacked motivation, and many of his school assignments were not completed on time and often, not completed at all.

Chance was a handsome boy, quite tall and rather chubby. He was polite, outspoken and very confident. He had large eyes, bushy eyebrows and a straight nose. His parents were relatively wealthy, but his standard of dressing did not mirror the affluence of his family.

"Would you like to join Phineas and me for lunch at the café?" Chance asked.

"I would have love to guys, but I am behind on my assignment for the next class. Maybe another day," replied Mark.

"All right, let's walk home together when classes are finished," Chance said as he grabbed his bag and the two walked out. Mark's reluctance to join Chance and Phineas was in part because he didn't have any money in his pocket. When he was called out of class by the headmaster a few days earlier, everyone in his class thought he had misbehaved and was curious to know what he had done. Mark explained that the Headmaster was checking his personal details. However, the word got out that he was behind with his school levy payments and he was embarrassed.

Mark also wanted to finish writing his notes following Mr Middleton's speech and to jot down a few questions to ask him. He needed more information on how he could draw up his personal principles and apply them in his life. As soon as he finished his notes, he took his lunch box from his bag and started eating.

When the school day ended, Mark did not get the chance to meet Mr Middleton who, after talking to the headmaster, proceeded straight into another meeting. So Mark joined Chance and Phineas, and the three walked home together.

"My father has gone on a business trip, and he won't be home until next week. I was hoping he would help me with my assignment. Tonight, I will ask my mum to help me. The task

Steps in the Middle

looks complicated. What's your assessment?" asked Chance.

"Yeah, it does look complicated. My dad is on leave this week, and so I'll get him to assist me after dinner tonight. My dad is good at mathematics," Phineas added proudly.

"We'll have to do our best. Perhaps we can compare our answers in the morning before we submit," Mark suggested.

"As for me," Phineas went on, "I don't have to struggle with assignments; my dad is more than willing to help me. My elder brother is a teacher, and he often helps me too. Sometimes I forget to ask them for help. Last month, I was struggling to finish my assignments, and I missed one this week too."

Chance interrupted him. "Why didn't you finish, Phineas, was the assignment so difficult? I can help you if you need assistance."

Phineas replied, "No, I never even attempted it. I slept late after watching the Euro soccer championship and then I forgot to ask Dad for help. My brother also came home early, but I also forgot to ask him. After the match, I dozed off on the couch, and I was only woken the next morning. The teacher twice wrote letters to Dad about it, and I explained to him that I had forgotten about the assignment. These days my dad asks me every day when I get home, so I rely on him to remind me sometimes," Phineas continued.

"How did he react when he saw the letters? Wasn't he angry with you?" Chance asked.

"At first he was heartbroken, and I apologised, but when I brought the second one, he didn't react as much. I promised him that I would not forget again but still, I kept on forgetting," Phineas replied.

"What about you?" Chance asked Mark.

"I haven't missed a deadline for submitting any assignment. I try to complete the tasks on my own. If there's time, I go to

Claremont library to do research before writing the assignment. I like to give myself enough time to research assignments before I write to ensure good quality work," replied Mark.

"So you mean your father doesn't help you, not even the previous assignment in which you were the highest in class? Did you research and do the assignment alone?" Chance asked, looking surprised.

"Yes, I write my assignments on my own, but I try to research before writing anything," Mark replied, trying to avoid any reference to his family. He felt uneasy with the direction the conversation was going. He particularly didn't want to talk about his father. His situation was quite different from that of his friends, who relied on parental support to complete their assignments. Mark didn't want them to know that his father was deceased and that he was living with his uncle, whom he had begged for accommodation so that he could attend a better school in Southwark.

"Oh, man! You are a hard worker," Chance exclaimed. "I can't imagine doing my assignments on my own without Dad. Even my sisters get assistance from him. Usually, when I get home, I just tell Dad that I have an assignment and he sets aside time to work it through with me. When he is not available; my elder brother also helps me."

Mark envied his friends' dependence on their parents for most their needs. They didn't have to struggle with anything; their future appeared guaranteed. When they got closer to home, Chance asked if he could accompany Mark to his home. Mark declined unsure of Beauty's reaction, but Chance insisted, and so they walked up to the gate before parting.

When Mark entered the gate, Beauty was outside having a close conversation with another woman. From the gate, he couldn't see clearly the other person until he got closer. Suddenly, he recognised Agnes, and his heart leapt with excitement as he hadn't seen her for some months. Agnes, who was expecting Mark's arrival from school at that time, opened her arms wide to him. "Oh Mark, my grandson, look how tall you are now!" she cried out and embraced him. They talked about everything that had happened since Mark's departure from Casterbridge while Beauty sat quietly in her chair.

Suddenly the weather changed, the wind picked up and dark clouds enveloped the sky. Soon torrential rains accompanied by hailstones, the size of golf balls pounded the rooftop while lightning and thunder lit up the skies. The walls of the house vibrated in response to thunder, sending the frightened dogs and cats into hiding. Nature demonstrated its supremacy over humankind. The rain bucketed down, and soon the ground was saturated, the drains overflowed. As it was peak hour, the city's transport system was disrupted. The violent winds brought down trees and power lines. Hail damage became apparent immediately after the rain. Some areas experienced power blackouts and flooded roads and sidewalks.

The storm had abated when Conrad's car pulled into the garage. As he walked into the house, Beauty seemed surprised to see Conrad so early that evening. "Mum, I wasn't expecting you!" he exclaimed. "How did you get here?" She and Beauty were seated around the dining room table. He walked forward to hug her before sitting down. Conrad looked at Beauty, and he muttered something inaudible which Beauty ignored. She looked coldly at him before dragging herself to the kitchen to fetch his meal from the oven. Beauty placed his plate in front of him without a word. Conrad remained motionless, his appetite vanished. This was not the kind of scene he wanted his mother to witness.

For a moment, it became quiet in the room, except for the sound of water running down the gutters from the roof.

Agnes and Beauty continued to eat from their plates, neither wanting to break the silence. Conrad's children had already disappeared like squirrels into their rooms when they first heard their father's voice. Occasionally, their giggles could be heard from their rooms. Conrad stood up and went to his bedroom, leaving Agnes and Beauty at the table. It was unusual for Agnes to travel to Southwark without his knowledge; in times past she had always asked for his assistance in travelling long distances. This time, Agnes was in Claremont without Conrad's knowledge or help. Suddenly, he became suspicious that Beauty had asked Agnes to come and mediate in their feud.

When Conrad emerged from his bedroom, Agnes and Beauty had finished dinner, and Conrad's plate was still on the table. He ignored it and took a seat on his favourite couch in the living room. Beauty and Agnes joined him in the living room. Conrad asked his mother, "Do you have the dates for this year's Catholic Convention and is it going to be in Casterbridge again?" He smiled to hide the tension in the room, but when he looked at Beauty, his smile vanished. Beauty looked away from him as if to say,

"Why do you care about that when you can't even care for your wife and family?"

Agnes responded to Conrad, pretending to be oblivious of Beauty's reaction. "The dates have not been announced yet, but the congregation has been told that it may well be in Casterbridge again. This is good news for me because I don't like travelling long distance anymore. Patrick will be taking me to the convention this time," replied Agnes.

After another moment of silence, Agnes continued, "I am in

Steps in the Middle

Claremont this time of the year because of you." Conrad experienced a flash of anger as he realised his suspicion had been confirmed. Beauty noticed Conrad's reaction to his mother's words. Agnes paused for a moment as if she didn't know how to continue the conversation. Her thoughts went back to many years earlier when she had confronted Conrad about his behaviour and how he had reacted then. Conrad had just finished high school at Bristol High, and after he had arrived home, he went to spend his vacation with Patrick, his brother, who was working in Seaford at the time. Patrick was married to Margaret, and the two had a young family. Margret's sister, Abigail, who was also on vacation, joined her sister in Seaford to help with the children.

When Conrad first met Abigail at Margaret's house, they seemed to have no mutual interests at all. They only talked when Patrick and Margaret were at home, after which each one of them preferred to be alone in their rooms. As days turned to weeks, the two began to warm up toward each other. They started taking the children to the park together, and during this time they enjoyed plenty of time to discover their mutual interests. One day, they went the beach, and while the children played with their toys on the sand, Conrad and Abigail went into the water. Conrad began teaching Abigail to swim. As they went deeper, the waves came crashing against them, and she became increasingly nervous. Conrad held her hand and slowly urged her even deeper into the water until their bodies were submerged to shoulder level. Abigail held tightly on to Conrad with her arms wrapped around his chest. They began to laugh wildly, and suddenly they realised that they were enjoying the closeness of each other's bodies.

Conrad felt the softness of Abigail's breasts, the smoothness of her skin, and he realised how beautiful she was. Abigail kept clinging to him. She began to enjoy the way Conrad was holding her. After some time, the two came out of the water holding hands, their eyes glowing with excitement. After a few weeks, Margaret became alarmed at the closeness between Conrad and Abigail, and by that time it was too late; the two had already crossed all the bridges. Three months afterwards, Abigail wrote to Conrad informing him that she was pregnant. When Agnes got wind of the news, she sat down with Conrad and told him sternly that he had to take responsibility for everything that had happened.

Back to the present, Conrad listened attentively at his mother as she addressed him. "Beauty has explained to me the problems you are having. She has told me that you are at work until late every day. Sometimes you stay out all night. You don't have time for your children. You come home when they are already asleep if you ever come and you no longer enjoy a meal together anymore. You have not spoken affectionately to her in many months and many other things. What have got to say about this?" Agnes paused and looked at Conrad with searching eyes. Conrad looked uncomfortable and humiliated.

"Can you explain to me what is going on right now?" Agnes persevered. "I am not going to allow you to talk your way out if it. Give me a straight answer."

Agnes paused and frowned. Conrad realised that his mother was serious. He said, "Mother, I'm sorry that you had to come all the way from Casterbridge to attend to my marital issues with Beauty. You have shown love and concern for us, and I appreciate your effort. I am going to tell you my side of the story, and if I'm wrong, you can correct me. Yes, Beauty and I have been arguing about some issues for months. She suspects that when I come home late, it is because I was with another woman. She accuses me of cheating on her and many other things. I run a business, part time and so every evening I carry out random checks on my business before I come home, and that's why I get home late. Casterbridge is quite a distance from Southwark to travel after hours and back. When I get home, I am tired because of travelling, and so I prefer to sleep early. I am very sorry if she feels that I am ignoring her but that is not my intention and everything is all right with us."

"No, that is not true! That is not true! Conrad is lying," Beauty interrupted.

"Yes, I have not spoken to Conrad for more than a month and when he comes from work he doesn't talk to me or his children. It's true that he doesn't play with the children. When I ask him where he's been, he refuses to answer. The children are afraid of him. When they see him, they run to their rooms. Ask him what kind of father he is? The children get ill, and he doesn't even know or check on the children because he is never home in time to see them to bed. I go to sleep asking myself where is he and when will he come back? But it's not because of his work. Sometimes he comes home so drunk that he sleeps on his couch, and I ask myself how he can drive all the way home from wherever he was, only to sleep on the couch. Why is it difficult for him to move from the couch to his bed if he can drive alone, park correctly in the garage and then walk indoors? I am tired of his behaviour." Tears ran down her cheeks.

"No, Beauty that is not fair. I am trying to secure a future for our children. I work hard to make enough money for their education. Just the other day, I gave you money to buy new clothes for the children. I asked you to take them to the movies, and they enjoyed it." Conrad's voice rose in anger.

Beauty turned to Agnes and said bitterly, "Conrad's top priority may be his work, but his family comes last. If his family were important to him, he would make an effort to be with us. The adage that, 'everyone has time and money for what they value most,' is so true in the case of Conrad. Conrad enjoys earning money and spending it with his friends. He doesn't want me to take a job. Whatever I do, outside the walls of this house makes him feel threatened. We don't just want his money, and it doesn't matter how much money he earns. We want to feel valued by him. We need his time too. We have feelings, and we need his time more than anything else. Money can be earned but time can never be earned, and that is what we are yearning for from his. Providing a family is not all about financial support, although we appreciate his financial support."

In the children's bedrooms, Chester and his siblings heard the loud voices as their parents' continued to argue well into the night. Meanwhile, the kids sounded distressed and unhappy as prepared to retire in bed in the midst of arguments going on in the living room. This wasn't common since nobody dared argue with Conrad.

Mark remained awake throughout the conversation which lasted almost the entire night, listening attentively to both sides of the argument. The anguish in Beauty's voice was apparent. Conrad didn't deny that he regularly comes home late, but he insisted that it was because of work. Mark wondered why his uncle, who had a beautiful wife, could even consider cheating on her. "How can a man provide all material necessities for his wife, yet fail to establish a fruitful relationship with her? Is it the woman's fault, and if it's her fault what does a woman want? Why can't she appreciate the material things she receives from a husband who has the means to provide and live contentedly?" Mark asked himself. But listening to Beauty, the question was answered succinctly. She argued that she wanted him to value her. She needed Conrad's attention more than the material possessions he brought. Until then, Mark thought the most important thing people wanted in life was money. Mark began to realise that happiness was less related to money than to one's emotional state.

CHAPTER 14

The mentors and the trip to Penrith

Whatever the outcome of the discussion Agnes had with Conrad and Beauty that night, the result was clearly evident in the morning. The victory was achieved, resulting in peace and harmony in the family. Conrad rose early to check on the children, and to the surprise of Mark, he even knocked on his door to check on him before heading off to work. This unusual behaviour surprised Mark and the children, who needed more time to be accustomed to his new behaviour. That morning the children struggled to get accustomed to the changed attitude of Conrad, they all responded to him cautiously as if they suspected him of sinister motive. Conrad found his behaviour strange and struggling to live by his promise from the first day. But Beauty was delighted to hear the kids telling her about the surprise early morning visit from Conrad.

The news from the children that morning was all Beauty

Steps in the Middle

needed to bring a glow back to her face. That morning, Conrad and Beauty took breakfast together while Agnes got ready to leave for Casterbridge. Their differences had been resolved in the early hours of the morning, apologies were given, and new commitments were made. It was thanks to Agnes that a new air graced the family. Conrad started coming back home early from the next day. He reduced his business trips and cut down his drinking parties. He stopped staying overnight without notifying Beauty. Beauty and the children's lives became better, and so did living conditions for Mark.

On the last day of school, Chance, Mark and Phineas walked home together talking about their vacation plans. Chance said, "I may be home the whole vacation, or we may travel abroad to the Austrian Alps for skiing. My dad loves skiing and every school vacation he takes us somewhere. Last time we went to Dundee and Aberdeen, and we enjoyed historical sites and museums."

Mark response was subdued. "There is nothing much that I can look forward to this holiday. I'm going to Casterbridge to be with my sisters and grandma. It has been some months since I last saw them."

Chance asked him, "Why don't you ask your parents to take you on holiday? It's such a good time to learn new things; just ask your dad to take you somewhere interesting."

"Yeah, I will," Mark replied, avoiding further discussion on the topic.

"Phineas, what's on your cards this vacation?" Chance enquired.

"We'll go camping. My father bought a new car, a four-wheel drive, it's beautiful. He has spoiled us with new toys," Phineas replied as they got closer to home.

Mark left for Casterbridge, excited at the prospect of being with his sisters again. When he arrived, Agnes was not at home. Martha and Masculine were in the kitchen busy preparing lunch; apparently, they were now able to cook unsupervised. Mark was surprised how much his sisters had grown. He hugged them, and they all sat down to talk. "Where is Agnes?" he asked. "Grandma has gone to church; she will be back soon," Martha replied.

She peeped through the window. "She has just arrived," she added. Mark ran out to embrace her.

"When did you arrive?" Agnes enquired.

"Just a few minutes ago," replied Mark.

"Have you eaten anything?" she asked.

"Grandma, Mark has just arrived. We haven't even offered him anything to eat yet," Martha interrupted.

Agnes looked at Mark with admiration. "You are growing up fast," she said. "You are so tall and strong. Soon you will be a fully grown man."

"Martha and Masculine are growing up fast too. They will soon be looking after you in return," said Mark.

"I don't tell your sisters what to do in this house anymore, they organise themselves and do all the chores and we all enjoy a meal without me getting involved in the kitchen. God is great," Agnes continued, pointing her finger to the ceiling. "I am getting old. I can't do much with my hands. Your sisters are a blessing to me. Without them, I would have been lonely in this house. Who would cook for me? Perhaps my sons would have already put me in a home for the elderly. Old Age Homes as people call them are not exciting places to spend the remainder of your life in. They are a depressing way of looking after the elderly. I think they should be used as the last resort. I want to live and die in my house." Agnes spoke with feeling.

"All right, Grandma, no one will put you in a home. We will look after you," Mark interjected.

Agnes stood up and went into her bedroom, and she came out with a letter which she handed to Mark. "Your mother wants you to travel to Penrith with your sisters. It has been long since you visited Larry and Matilda and I am sure they will be happy to see you three again. You can spend two weeks with them." Agnes paused looking at Mark.

"What about you, Grandma? Will you remain behind alone?" asked Martha.

"I will stay here with Dominic. We will be alright. If I need anything he can help me before he goes to work," replied Agnes.

When Bothwell heard that Mark was back from Southwark, he and his brothers came over to Agnes's house right away and soon they were playing at the back of the house. Bothwell was happy to see Mark and exchanged news about their respective schools, their teachers and their school curricula. As evening approached, Mark walked Bothwell back home. On his way back, he noticed Mr Wood walking toward his house. Mark ran to meet him. Looking surprised, Mr Wood stopped and asked "Who are you? I can't recognise you. I left my spectacles at home." Mr Wood looked old. He had lost weight, and his grey hair hung down from his black straw hat. He wiped his face with a grey handkerchief from his pocket. "Are you Agnes's grandson?"

"Yes, Mr Wood. Have you forgotten me?" replied Mark.

"Oh, I am so sorry, my friend. You have grown so tall. Agnes told me that you live in Southwark now, is that right?" asked Mr Wood.

"Yeah, I just arrived back home today. I was going to come and see you tomorrow," replied Mark.

"Do you have anything specific in mind to discuss?"

"No, not really; I have been thinking about what you told me, that I am responsible for my success. At first, I didn't believe that it was true, but now I think you were right," replied Mark.

"Why don't you walk with me to my house?" Mr Wood asked. "Look here Mark, I want to tell you a few things about life," he continued just as they were inside the house. "There a few lessons that I have learnt in my life, which I can share with you if you have a moment. Most people fail, not because they don't have anything to start with. They already have nearly everything they need, but instead of getting on with it, they spend too much time moaning and groaning about what they don't have. Some years ago, I inherited a piece of land from my grandfather, which he hadn't used for many years. That portion of land was arid and dry, but the other plots next to it had access to water.

For many years, I complained about being unable to grow crops because of the lack of water. The land was situated on the slopes of a hill, and it is hard to drill a borehole because of the rock around it. After seven years of lying fallow, I decided to sell it. But before I could sell it, I thought of dividing it into smaller lots after which I spread the word. Suddenly many people were interested. But then one man offered to buy the land undivided, to which I agreed, and he handsomely paid me. To my surprise, he started breeding sheep. I doubted his wisdom for a while, knowing that there was no access to water. Then after a few months, I learnt that he was using a tractor every two days, to refill troughs located at specific points on the piece of land. It was a simple solution to the problem, and yet I had never thought of it. He developed the plot further, and now his farm is the largest supplier of mutton in the whole of Casterbridge.

Steps in the Middle

There is still no borehole on the property, even today. I had eighty percent of what I needed for a project like that, but I lamented over the twenty percent I didn't have, and as a result, I lost the opportunity. Some mistakes in life cost too much, and when you make them, you will never be able to correct them," he paused.

"It may be the same with you," he went on. "Don't moan over the death of your father; it has already happened. It is now water under the bridge. Look at your present circumstances and focus on what is working in your favour. You already have much of what you need. Your biggest challenge is to think of a plan that delivers something of value to other people, using your limited resources available to you. People are always prepared to pay for some things that make their life easier and solves a problem. In that way there will be an exchange; you will get what you want and your customers likewise. In the journey of life, ideas are more important than gold. Don't wish you had more money, but rather hope for more ideas.

Nothing is easy and so don't wish it was easy too but wish for more ideas. If you have ideas, you can always make more money. Many people think that they are poor because they don't have money, yet in reality, their poverty is partly caused by their lack of courage to make ideas work for them. Anyone with a good idea will find a way of obtaining gold. A man who is creative will always find something which solves a problem, and people will be happy to pay him for it, and his purse will never run dry," he said paused for a moment.

"On the other hand, whiners will always look for reasons why things are difficult for them. For most whiners, life is a burden. They magnify little problems by exaggerating the facts, so as to solicit unwarranted sympathy. They always believe other people are the cause of their difficult life and never their actions. They like to hold other people accountable but never themselves, and they dream of making money one day, while they never sit down to work on anything. Their talk is about what they would like to do one day, and that day never arrives. Money is attracted to people with ideas, and never those who wish is to have it for the sack of having it. If a man without an idea happens to get money by mere chance, it won't be long before he loses it all. That is exactly what happened to me; I thought that by selling the land, I would be rich and I wouldn't need to work again. I was wrong, and I missed the point of having money. Without ideas, alas the money quickly disappeared from my purse hardly a year after I sold the land," he paused to sip from his cup.

"Some people are like frogs. If you put a frog in a jar of cold water and the water is boiled slowly, the frog will boil to death. That is how whiners react; they keep trying to adjust to their environment and they never shape the environment. They spend a lot of time complaining about their lot in life while they do nothing to change the situation until they die. On the other hand, if you take a frog and put it in a jar of hot water, the frog will immediately jump out. That's how creative people react to opportunities. They are quick when they see opportunities. Look at those hot coals," Mr Wood pointed to the red hot coals burning in the fireplace.

"If I ask you to grab some of the coals in your hand and place them in the cold water next to the fireplace, do you think you can do it?" he paused.

"No, I don't think I can," replied Mark smiling.

"Yes, that proves my point. If you think you can't do something, you won't be able to do it. In life, if you believe you can do something, you will almost always succeed, but if you think

Steps in the Middle

you can't do it, you will most likely fail. If you convince yourself that it is possible, your body and mind will collaborate to deliver your desired outcome. If you keep working on the task, you will eventually have a breakthrough. When I married Kate, she was a fitness fan. Every morning, she ran two miles before starting her day. One day I decided to surprise Kate by joining her for the run. Even though I wasn't particularly in bad shape, my body was not used to exercising, and so I had to stop because my legs were hurting, my knees were wobbly, my heart was beating fast, and my throat was dry. But I was determined to make Kate happy, and within a few weeks, I could run many miles alongside Kate without difficulty. If you believe you can achieve your goal, work hard at it day and night, maintain the right attitude, and you will certainly make it. That applies to your success at school as well."

Mr Wood looked at his watch and said, "It's getting late. You ought to go home now. We can continue another day when you have time."

Mark leapt from his seat, thanked Mr Wood and hastened down the street. He respected Mr Wood's words of wisdom which were just what he needed in the absence of a father. "I am lucky to have someone like him to guide me. Next time, I will bring a notebook so that I can write down what he tells me," Mark said to himself as he ran back home. "Mr Wood looks at me as if I have already succeeded; it makes me feel great. I love to listen to him," thought Mark. From that day, people noticed with appreciation the relationship between the two unlikely age groups.

Mr Wood later came to Agnes's house. "I am here to talk you about Mark," he began. Agnes listened attentively. "I have been spending a lot of time with your grandson. He has shown interest in being taught about life, and I must say that I have found him very inquisitive and eager to learn. He wants to succeed, and I have been doing my best to satisfy his curiosity. Has he mentioned that to you? If not, I thought you should know about our conversations with him, in case you may feel otherwise." Mark was not at home at the time; he only learnt that Mr Wood had visited Agnes when he arrived back home. Days later Mark came looking for Mr Wood, in his hand was a notebook and a pen, intending to record Mr Wood's wisdom. At the gate, he met Lily, Mr Wood's daughter and behind her was Mr Wood, looking tired and drained.

"I am sorry, Mark, we are going to the doctor. Mr Wood is not feeling well; I think he has the flu. He has lost his voice, and there behind me, he is coming. So you won't be able to have your lecture today. He will be all right soon. Give him a couple of days, and his voice will be back again," Kate spoke optimistically. Mark waved at Mr Wood and walked out, shutting the gate behind him. "I wonder if he has taught his daughter to be optimistic too?" thought Mark. "She has a lot of confidence; her attitude is as good as his."

Mark was unable to have another meeting with Mr Wood before travelling to Penrith with his sisters. It had been some years since he was last in Penrith with his mother, and he had no idea how to locate Larry's house. As they sat in the coach, he felt compassion for his sisters who were looking tired. He wished he had a car so he could drive directly to Larry's house.

Remembering Mr Wood's words about having a positive attitude, he said to himself, "One day I will have a car. Keeping a positive attitude is not easy, and I must stop saying that I don't have sufficient resources to achieve my ambitions. If you have an idea, you will work out for yourself what resources you need, where and how to get them. This is what I did when I focused on achieving top marks in junior school. Now I am focusing on completing my high school with good grades again. I need to become successful so that I can buy my mother a house and help her support my sisters. How many years do I need to work to get money to purchase a home? Oh, that's a difficult question to answer. But should I just keep this in my mind or tell people what I want to be when I grow up? What if they laugh at me? Maybe I just keep it to myself. It's hard to live with another family where one isn't free to express oneself. Anyway, thanks to Uncle Conrad that I can live with his family but sometimes it is painful living with them." Mark's reverie was interrupted when the coach driver called out, "Next stop, Penrith!"

Mark woke up Martha and Masculine from dreamland. The girls had started off the trip excited and happy to be on their first trip away from Casterbridge, wide-eyed at the passing scene. But as the coach trip dragged on, fatigue set in and they nodded off in their seats. On arrival at the station, Mark said, "Penrith looks much bigger now. Look at that high-rise building and the other one behind it; they are all new. But some things have changed," he shouted to his sisters pointing in all the directions.

"There is the farmers' market; it is still at the same place, it was years ago. I used to come with Matilda to the market to buy vegetables. Farmers from surrounding areas would come here to sell their fresh produce every day. Look over there; Larry used to work at those offices." Mark pointed at the office block north of the market place as he seemed mesmerised by how some things had changed in Penrith. He looked at Martha and Masculine who appeared restless. "What is the matter?" he asked. "Can I get you something to eat?"

"Yes," they nodded in unison. They found a restaurant a few

blocks away from the market, and they sat down to eat. Mark said, "I lived in Penrith for a long time after Dad died. I stayed with Larry and his wife, Matilda. You won't remember them; you left Penrith when you were too young. They are a very nice couple, and I am sure you will enjoy meeting them. We will be with them for two weeks." They both looked nervous. Even Masculine, usually jumping around, pointing at things and asking many questions, appeared reticent. Martha, on the other hand, was a quiet girl, rarely speaking and more reserved than the younger sister. As he walked out of the restaurant holding their hands, he also felt a little uneasy.

They walked down the street, and people gazed at the unknown trio. Mark and his sisters felt strange and unfamiliar too. Then Larry's house came into view. "We are going to that white house. Can you see it?" Mark exclaimed, pointing to Larry's house. Nearby was a recreational park where children were playing, their parents keeping watch over them. Masculine said excitedly, "Look at that little girl swinging. Can I go there?"

"No, not now, Masculine, we must go to Larry's house first then I will take you to the park to play later," replied Mark.

As they reached Larry's house, Mark noticed that the gate was closed and the house apparently deserted. There were cracks in the walls, and the paint had faded. Rank weeds had grown around the house. The windows were uncurtained, and the door handles rusted. Mark was puzzled, from where he was standing, he called out for Larry, but there was no answer. "Am I lost? Is this not grandfather's house? Where is he then?" he asked himself. They sheltered under a tree to avoid the intense heat. Mark tried to remember where Matilda's friend, Rose Henderson lived. Then a woman, who had been watching them as they approached Larry's house called out. "Hello! If you're looking for the people who used to live there, they left a long time ago."

Mark and his sisters walked silently in the direction of the woman, before greeting her. "I am Mark, and these are my sisters Martha and Masculine. We have come to be with our grandparents for two weeks, but we are all surprised they aren't there. It looks like they don't live there anymore. Do you know where they have moved to?"

The woman replied. "We are new in this area. We moved in recently, but we never met the elderly man who used to live there. I understand there is an older woman who lives further down this road was known to him. Maybe she can help."

Mark immediately felt distressed. He considered returning to Casterbridge, but it was too late in the day to secure a ticket back to Casterbridge. He didn't have money to pay for lodging for himself and his sisters for the night. The woman understood his concern. "Mark," she said, "Why don't you go to the friend I was telling you about. I will give you directions to her house. If she can't help, I can give you accommodation tonight and then you can be on your way tomorrow," the woman continued.

"Thank you very much, I am sure we will find Larry today," replied Mark.

"I am not sure about that," the woman replied as if she knew something more than she had revealed. On hearing those words, Mark paused for a moment, he wanted to ask more questions, but something stopped him. Mark went back to look at the house again, the windows on Larry's bedroom and the tree under which Larry used to have a barbeque, all looked familiar. The paddocks were empty; there was no hay in the barn and roof of the barn had collapsed. In the fields, there were no crops anymore nor had there been a harvest the previous season. The ban looked rundown, and so was the house, and everything around it. Mark was sure that he was at the same place that he had lived with Larry and Matilda years earlier. Surely his grandfather wouldn't have moved without telling anyone where he was relocating to. Besides Larry's was a well-known person in Penrith. Rank weeds had grown around the house, as far as the doorstep. "This is my grandfather's house; I am not lost. I lived here before," Mark thought.

The woman scribbled something on a piece of paper and handed it to Mark saying, "Here is the address." Mark summoned his courage, led his sisters and walked off with a new determination. He had to find where Larry and Matilda had relocated to, before nightfall. Martha and Masculine looked weary. "Come," he said. "Let's find the house, and you can then rest. Don't worry; everything will be all right," Mark assured his sisters as they walked down the street in grave silence. Occasionally dogs barked as they combed the streets looking for the address.

The weather cooled off as the afternoon lengthened. Mark dreaded the thought of staying overnight at the house of the woman who had just assisted them with directions. For a while, he kept looking at his purse as if he was considering another option. All he had left in the purse was enough for the bus fare back to Casterbridge. The woman had shown kindness, but Mark remained uneasy with her. She looked strange to him, her excessive jewellery and tattoos all over much of her visible body scared the wits out of him. When Mark looked at her face, he couldn't maintain eye contact with her. Martha and Masculine, on seeing her makeup and jewellery, stood a distance away from her but Mark braved it all to speak to her. Something was strange about her, but he could not place a finger on what it was.

Mark hurried down the road with his sisters, and soon Masculine couldn't keep pace. "What's wrong Masculine, are you tired?" he asked. "Yes," she said looking down. Mark shrugged his shoulders and adjusted the straps of the bag behind his back. "Come, big brother will carry you." He lifted her and lifted her in his arms, and they continued down the road. It didn't take long before, Martha started trailing behind and struggling to keep up with Mark's strides, and so he reduced his pace. Martha asked, "Why do we have to come all this way to visit Larry and Matilda? Why is it that they don't come to visit us?" "I will explain when we seat down" replied Mark. He was beginning to worry about how far they still needed to walk before reaching Rose's house. He was becoming tired of carrying the bag strapped on his back.

When they reached Rose's address, an elderly woman was basking in the sun of the late afternoon. For a moment, Mark wasn't convinced that the woman was Rose. She was seated on a garden chair in the hot sun and holding a stick in one hand. She paid no heed to Mark and his sisters as they approached. Her face was fixed on the ground as if she was in deep thought.

"Hello, Madam, my name is Mark, and these are my two sisters, Martha and Masculine," Mark introduced himself and his sisters. The woman raised her head. "Hello, where are you from?" She said.

"We are from Casterbridge. We came to Penrith today to visit our grandparents but we could find them at their old address. The house looks deserted, and a neighbour gave us your address, she said you might be able to help us find them. Do you know where they are living now?" asked Mark. The weight of the bag on Marks bag was beginning to make him uncomfortable. He expected to be given further directions to help him locate Larry and Matilda before sunset. He hoped the woman would give them Larry and Matilda new address without putting his bag down or delaying them. For a moment Mark and his sisters remained on their feet, hoping to continue their walk immediately.

Chapter 15

The mentor like no other

The old woman stood up and looked at Mark and his sisters, and she gave them the best smile she could. Immediately she called out for someone inside the house to bring chairs. Three chairs were brought, and glasses of cold water followed. Mark became worried as he didn't want to take a rest until he had found Larry and Matilda. He doubted whether it was a good idea to take a seat before they reached their final destination. He noticed that the woman was trying hard to be courteous, but he was more interested in expediency than courtesy. Meanwhile, he sought to indicate by signs that he didn't want to seat down and the elderly woman continuing for a moment in silence without paying attention to him.

The woman's face was wrinkled, and her hands were cracked and dry. She appeared tired and worn out. Forcing a smile, she said, "I am Rose Henderson, do you remember me?" Mark's face lit up when he heard the name 'Rose'. He remembered Mrs Henderson's name from long ago when he was still young, but he couldn't recognise her that moment because the picture he had in his mind of Rose, wasn't of a wrinkled old lady.

"Yes, I remember your name, Mrs Henderson," replied Mark. "It has been some years since I left Penrith. I am glad to meet you again. Do you remember my sisters?" He pointed at Martha and Masculine.

"Yes, I am glad to meet you all again. I thought I would never see you again in my lifetime," Rose replied. "You know, I was a friend of your mother and father. When your father died, my husband and I became friends to Larry and Matilda too." Rose recalled the death of Gabriel, his burial and the wartime events like it was just yesterday. She spoke slowly, pausing now and then to sip from her glass of water. Within a few moments in her discourse, Martha and Masculine fell asleep on their chairs. Rose called for her granddaughters to take them inside and Mark stood up to help them. The guest room was spacious and comfortable. Martha and Masculine were placed on the freshly-prepared bed and carefully covered with an expensive quilt.

Mark returned outside to continue his conversation with Rose. He was relieved that Rose was able to accommodate them for the night, should they not be able to locate Larry and Matilda. She didn't seem to be in a hurry to give them directions to Larry's house, but the warmth in her voice struck a code with Mark.

"They are tired of walking. I showed them several different places in town before we got to Larry's house. The girls are not used to walking, so today was rather difficult for them," Mark said as he resumed his seat.

"Listen, Mark, maybe you are too young for me to give you

all the details of what happened to your grandparents, but since you have come to visit them, there's no way I can avoid telling you what took place. It is even difficult for me to explain; they were my friends. We shared many good times together. Over six months ago Larry's health began to deteriorate. I could see that he had lost weight and when I asked him about it, he just told me he was all right. One night he went to sleep and didn't wake up the next morning. I was told that Larry had passed on to the great darkness. A year before he died, he and Matilda had divorced. Larry was now living alone and as you know this can be difficult for an elderly man after many years of having a companion."

Rose paused and took a sip from her glass again. She was really in no hurry to go over any conversation. She continued speaking and pausing every so often, pronouncing each word from her mouth carefully. Mark was incredulous. "Do you mean grandfather died more than six months ago?" he asked.

Rose looked at Mark and said in a soft voice, "Larry is no longer among the living; his soul rests in peace somewhere. If I'm feeling well, I will take you and your sisters to the cemetery tomorrow and show you his grave. There were many people at his funeral; they came from, far and wide. Larry was the well-known person in Penrith. Julius and Peter, their wives and children, travelled overnight from Roselle to attend his funeral. After his burial, I stayed at his house for a few days helping out. As you saw, the house is still unoccupied till today. I sent messages to Julius and Peter to find someone to rent the house, but I haven't heard any response from them. Larry's house will soon be unfit for occupation. I don't understand why your uncles seem reluctant to put it up for rental or sale; there are so many people looking for accommodation."

Mark said, "No one told us of Larry's death. Certainly, we wouldn't have made this journey today. We would also have attended his funeral. Mum arranged this trip for us, hoping that we would enjoy the company of Larry and Matilda for two weeks. I guess we will have to travel back home tomorrow after visiting the cemetery."

"You don't have to rush back to Casterbridge so soon," Rose spoke reassuringly. "I am happy for you and your sisters to spend some days with us if that idea is alright with you since you are on vacation. There are so many things to do in Penrith, and you can take the time to show your sisters around."

Mark wasn't sure how his sisters would feel staying at Rose's house. Maybe they would not get on well with her granddaughters. However, to reassure him, he heard laughter. Martha and Masculine had woken up. Mark looked round and saw them running up and down with Rose's granddaughters in the play area, where there were many toys and games. Rose lived with her three grandchildren, daughters of her youngest son. Two of them were the same age as Martha and Masculine, and the eldest was a little older than Mark.

"Let's all go indoors; it's getting dark. You can play again tomorrow," Rose called, and soon everyone was indoors.

From outside, Rose's house was not the most attractive, yet the interior compensated for its modest external appearance. The house was fitted with exotic carpets, smart furniture and fine lamps. Photographs of Rose's children and grandchildren at various stages of their lives were hung on the walls as well as photographs of her wedding day. On display were also trophies given to her husband, some of which she could hardly remember why they had been presented to him. Mark spent a moment looking at Rose's wedding photographs before he took his seat. "That was taken at Brentwood Park many years ago," said Rose. In the photograph, she was clothed in a snow-white wedding dress, standing tall and confident, radiating good health and beauty.

"You were a beautiful bride," Mark remarked.

"Yeah, it's a pity; we can't stay like that for ever," replied Rose. "Life is like a flower; when it is planted, we look forward flowers budding and blossoming. Then after that, we wait for the seeds to be formed, after that the plant withers. In the same way, when you are young, you look forward to growing up and blossoming. When you get old, you look back and thank heavens that you are still alive." Rose went on to describe her wedding day and the arrival of her first child.

Catherine, her eldest granddaughter, walked in and announced dinner. While she was preparing dinner in the kitchen, she had the attention of the girls, telling stories and keeping them amused. "Let's us go in," said Rose. She struggled to her feet. It was clear Rose's body was ailing and her health deteriorating. She was no longer the same person Mark knew from years ago.

After dinner Rose shuffled into the living room and sank comfortably into her favourite couch, from which she had a full view of everyone walking in and out of the living room. "Sit down there, Mark," Rose said, pointing to the couch next to her. "Let me finish the story of your grandparents. As you know, Matilda had become an alcoholic long ago. Larry spent many years helping her to recover and for a while, she stopped drinking altogether. Then one day, Larry came back from a business trip and found Matilda drinking with friends. She was intoxicated beyond measure, and her relapse saddened Larry. Matilda couldn't put up with his continual entreaties to give up alcohol, and so she moved out of

Larry's house and went to live alone. Her drinking binges became worse putting her at odds with her new neighbours. When she became ill again, her cousins took her in, and that is the last I heard about her. She is living somewhere in Glebe." Rose paused.

Rose paused and wiped her mouth with a cloth. "You see, life is partly what happens to you and partly what you choose to do about it. What you decide to do makes the difference between success and failure. Every day we are confronted with situations where we are required to make decisions. Matilda always wanted to be drinking in the company of friends. She felt that this was her consolation for not having children. She tried everything she could to conceive but without success. Yes, a woman's pride is the sons of her womb, but she wasn't the first one to be barren.

Bad things happen to us all; things beyond our control but we cannot wish them away. Whatever happens in your life is for a reason; it teaches you a lesson. Learn from your past failures and those of others, and use your reflections to become better. Anyone who detests learning will fall into the same pit several times and will have many years of experience in falling in the same pit. Experience doesn't result in wisdom; it is only when one reflects and resolves to be better. Matilda failed to learn from her many near death experiences with alcohol abuse until Larry couldn't take it anymore. On the other hand, Matilda saw herself as a victim. She talked about her problems to get attention and not a solution. She called herself 'the unlucky one', 'the one born-to-fail' and many other names. She made friends with Lucy and Perpetua, who were in similar predicaments. Lucy was a divorcee who had been married for twenty years, and when her husband left her for a younger woman, she went into depression and tried to commit suicide three times. She met a man drinking in a pub, and he moved in with her. After a few months, he left her and Lucy's world collapsed again. She started ill-treating her children, and they moved out, and they went to live with their father.

Perpetua's story was a little different. She lost her job after working for her employer for fifteen years. She was dismissed for no apparent reason and fought a legal battle with her employer until all her savings were exhausted. At the end of it, she lost the case. She couldn't get another job, and she started selling farm produce at the market. This is where she met Lucy. They became friends and began spending considerable time together drinking in pubs."

Mark, thinking about his life, said: "Yes, but bad things also happen to good people."

Rose continued. "I was a social worker for many years, and I learnt a lot about life. Your father Gabriel passed on when you were still young, and your mother was already pregnant with Masculine; now you are all being raised by your grandmother, is that correct?"

"Yes, Grandma takes care of us because Mum is working away from home," replied Mark.

"The death of your father is similar to a story of people in a boat; tossed hither and thither by waves, causing it to break up. Whatever they decide to do after the vessel is broken into pieces, will determine where they will end up in life. They will have many choices facing them. They can panic about the broken boat, complain how unfair it is that the boat has broken, be sad about it and simply do nothing. They can also each choose to grab a piece of the boat and float their way in the direction of the shore. Whatever decision each one will choose, there will be a consequence.

Steps in the Middle

Even your life situation today is no different to that of Matilda, Lucy and Perpetua. Ask someone who has failed many times, what's the reason for their failure and take notes if you can? The notes will be a good example of what to avoid. Talk to someone who has succeeded and ask them why, and you will learn how to succeed. Reflecting on other people's experiences will help you avoid many pitfalls in life. The reflections can be the beginning of wisdom. As regards your life, don't spend time crying about Gabriel's death, you can't change that. The boat is already broken into pieces. Grab a piece of what is left and float your way to the dry ground. Success or failure has a recipe, whatever decision you make every day leads you to either outcome." Suddenly, Rose had become energetic and lively; she was speaking with force and experience. Her counsel was sinking deep into Mark's heart.

Rose continued. "You have the potential to achieve anything you want if you put your mind to it. Your mother might be working as a helper and struggling to earn enough money to pay school levies for you and your sisters. Money is not the most important thing you need to succeed. If you don't have enough money, make the best of what you already have working in your favour, and float your way to your destination. Don't focus on where you are coming from, how poor your family is and what you don't have. Focus on your destination; look out for the shoreline and float in that direction. Success comes from inspiration by others or from sheer desperation to improve your circumstances. Your family's financial situation is not unique. Even those with both parents struggle with other problems." She paused.

"But every day I suffer the shame of going to school without necessities, yet my classmates have wealthy parents who can provide whatever they need such as clothes, shoes, money to buy whatever they need, textbooks and all that. How do you explain that?" asked Mark.

"Are you telling me that these lucky students are achieving good grades as well?"

Mark thought about his friend Phineas and replied, "No. Some of the students who have all the textbooks don't like reading."

"Textbooks are simply tools to make it easier to succeed. If you don't have the required books, you can go to the library. All resources are useful when they are applied wisely. If you have clarity on what you want to achieve, you will find a way of getting whatever is missing. There is no reason why you can't pass your examinations as well as anyone else who has all the textbooks. Mark, what is your desire when you leave school?" Rose asked.

"I want to buy mother a house so that we don't have to live in shared accommodation, and I want to buy other properties so that I can rent them out and get money," replied Mark, expecting Rose to say that his ambitions were beyond reach.

Rose replied without hesitation, "Good, by the yard it is hard but inch by inch you will certainly get what you want. Keep before your eyes, that which your heart desires and start working your way toward it, one step at a time. Write down a plan of how you intend to achieve what you want and keep it before your eyes. It is now almost midnight. Let me show you where you will sleep. We will continue the discussion tomorrow. Catherine has already made arrangements for your sisters, and they are fast asleep now."

Rose struggled from her seat, walked down the passage and showed Mark his room for the night. "We'll find time to visit the cemetery when I wake up tomorrow," she said, before disappearing into her bedroom.

That night Mark did not sleep well, not because his bed was

uncomfortable but because of what Rose had said to him. Her way of looking at life was similar to that of Mr Wood. She had spoken with the same passion and conviction. She dismissed the notion that Gabriel's death should be a barrier to Mark's future success. She had persuaded him to believe that his family background was not nearly as important as his decisions and choices about the future. All he needed to do was to grab a piece of the 'broken boat and float to shore'.

Mark was convinced that Rose was speaking from experience. The moments he had spent with Rose had added many insights into his life and helped him discover himself. Mark no longer thought that sons inherit wisdom only from their fathers and that those without fathers were doomed to fail. Rose's short lecture that day had shredded all his limiting beliefs, and he was ready to re-write a fresh chapter in his life and start afresh.

When he arrived at Rose's house and saw her seated outside in the hot sun, he never thought she had such a wealth of wisdom. Her age and poor health gave a false impression of who she was. He had mistakenly judged Rose by her physical appearance. That night Mark thought of asking Rose if he could extend his stay to a week so that he could learn more from her. What's more, his sisters were enjoying themselves with their new friends, and that was a comfort to him. He would have been uneasy if his sisters were not enjoying their stay.

Mark was woken up by the sound of children playing behind the house. He jumped out of bed and peered through the window. His sisters and Catherine's young sisters, Dorothy and Doreen, were enjoying themselves in the children's play area. Their smiles and laughter clearly couldn't be contained.

Rose knocked on his door. "Mark, you'd better get up now.

We must go to the cemetery before it gets too hot." Rose had been a while, exercising outside the house. She only stopped when Catherine called her in for breakfast. Mark joined everyone in the kitchen for the meal.

They set off for the cemetery and arrived at Larry's grave before the heat of the sun was too intense. "This is the grave of your grandfather," said Rose, handing over flowers to Mark. He placed the flowers on Larry's grave as Rose instructed him. She stood at the foot of the grave for a moment with her head bowed down, praying silently and for a moment everyone remained quiet. There were no other people in the cemetery. There weren't many graves with fresh flowers or had there been any recent activity in the cemetery. Mark and his sisters had neither been to a cemetery before nor had they ever witnessed a burial ceremony. After a moment of silence, Rose pointed to the tombstone at the head of the grave. "See when he died; I don't have my reading glasses," said Rose. Mark read out the dates for the others to hear. "Your father's grave is not in this cemetery. I would have shown you if it was," Rose continued. She led them out the cemetery, and they headed home quietly.

Rose struggled to keep pace with the children. She was breathing heavily, and sweat was running down her forehead because of the heat. When Rose stopped to take a rest for the third time, she told Catherine and the other children to proceed without her. Mark remained with her. "I used to walk long distances when I was younger," she said. "Every morning, I exercise before breakfast, and that has kept me fit. I take short walks around the neighbourhood once every so often."

"Let us walk slowly, and we can stop again if you need to rest," said Mark.

"I have rested enough; let us go," Rose said. When they arrived home, Rose went straight to her bedroom, shut the door behind her and took a nap.

Mark was sitting alone on the patio when Catherine called him, "Come! Let's have lunch. Grandma always takes a nap at this time of the day. She won't be up until after an hour or two." It seemed that Catherine ran Rose's household and she knew everything about Rose's diet and medication. During the meal, Catherine revealed that she was three classes ahead of Mark. She was enrolled at a prestigious school north of Southwark and was due to complete her studies the following year. For three years she had topped her class, winning prizes and awards. Mark enquired with Catherine the secret of her success to which she responded, "I study hard during school hours and during vacations too. I don't have time to waste. I want to be a doctor, and I have to work hard to achieve my goal."

Catherine stood up and fetched her report book, gave it to Mark so he could read her teacher's comments. Mark was impressed; the remarks were all encouraging, and he felt inspired by Catherine's academic success. "Once I finish helping Grandma, I put my sisters to bed, go into my room and spend another two or three hours studying before I retire to sleep. I have trained myself not to go to bed before reading," said Catherine. Mark realised that Catherine was more determined than he was in achieving her goals. She knew exactly why she was studying; she wanted to be a doctor.

"What do you want to be after school?" asked Catherine.

"I haven't decided yet. My mother wants me to look for an office job," replied Mark.

"You want to work in an office as for what?" Catherine asked.

"Ah, I don't know the jobs I can do in the office. Maybe, I will become a teacher," Marked replied, clearly unsure of what his plans were and a little embarrassed by Catherine's questions.

"Do you have a plan for your school vacation? Do you have assignments that I can help you with? Did you bring your books with you? I can help you if you need any assistance on topics that I have already studied. I have many books which I no longer need. Would you like to take them back to Southwark?" Catherine's questions rained on Mark like hailstones. At first, he was too shy to admit that he was not as organised as Catherine but when he saw that he could learn from her, he opened up.

"I would certainly like your help with mathematics, but I didn't bring my textbooks here. I haven't figured out what jobs office people do, but I will understand that with time," replied Mark. Catherine's eagerness to help was encouraging but the more she asked him, the more he realised how little he knew about so many things.

She was herself a life student of Rose's. Despite their age difference, the two were very close friends. With the approval of her parents, she spent every school vacation with Rose. She said to Mark, "You have to decide beforehand what you want to do when you graduate from high school. Whatever you choose, it should be something you like doing; something that you have a passion for. It shouldn't just be what your mother suggested for you.

No one should have to follow up with you to fulfil your desire. If it is your passion, you'll never get tired of working on it. I brought my books to read during my vacation. Grandma doesn't have to follow up, to see if I am still working on my goal. I don't need anyone to supervise me. If I have a question, I ask for her guidance, but I already have a clear plan for my future, and I read it to Grandma the last weekend. You should write down your plan for the next day before you go to bed. This might be difficult at first, but it gets easier with time. Planning is important; it helps you to focus."

"Yesterday I told Rose that I want to buy my mother a house and also buy other properties to rent. Is that what you are talking about?" Mark asked.

"No, Mark. That is what you want to achieve. But how will you get the money to buy a house? You have to find something that you are passionate about. It can be a product or service which solves people's problems and for which they will be prepared to pay you. People don't just spend money for nothing; except of course in church or other places where people donate for a cause. Even at church, people who donate believe that their contribution is of greater value to themselves and the community they live in, and that is why they give. So when you are studying your books, don't read to pass the exam but to prepare for your future profession and passion."

"Catherine, you have Rose as to guide you; perhaps that is why you are doing well. As for me, I have no one to advise me," said Mark.

"Rose is my mentor, and her guidance is invaluable, and you are perfectly right to say that, but remember I had a written plan before I approached her. She helped me review my plan, but the plan is mine. I still have to plan my day, week and many years ahead. I am responsible for making it work. You must find someone who has succeeded in what you want to do and let them advise you. Listen to those who know the ropes; most experienced people are willing to help others. As for me, I visit Grandma every vacation because she inspires me. Perhaps, that's why Grandma and I are close."

"I can hear my name out there, who is that blessing me?" interrupted Rose as she emerged from her bedroom.

Catherine replied, "Yes, I was just talking about you, Grandma, and sharing with Mark some of the things you have taught me and how your advice has changed my life."

"I have not changed your life; no one can change you except yourself. Listen, anyone can change when they find a strong enough motive to do so. People dislike being changed by other people, and they often react negatively by resisting change. I have yet to see anyone who was changed by someone else. People change themselves when they begin to feel exasperated by a lack of progression in their lives, and sometimes some people are inspired by others to follow their passion. That is when change happens. The will of a person is one of the greatest forces in the universe. It can take a man beyond his limitations and help him reach the stars." Rose paused before stretching her arms.

Catherine had boundless energy; she skipped from one spot to another doing her chores. Mark admired her zeal for life and her confidence about the future. "Have you always been this confident, Catherine?" asked Mark.

"I think so," replied Catherine. "Being confident doesn't mean that I know everything; it just means that I do my best with all that I have and believe. In the same way, be sure to build your confidence about your prospects. Keep your hopes high and motivate yourself every day to do the best that you can. That is my slogan!" she said. "If you have sufficient confidence in yourself, you will ward off the burning arrows of your critics. Rose is good at reminding me about self-confidence. You must ask her to teach you while you are here."

"Gabriel was a hardworking man," Rose interjected. "Maria

was my friend, but she was much younger than me. When your father died, I stayed with Maria for some months consoling her. Remember yesterday; I gave you the analogy of a boat on the high seas hitting a rock and breaking into pieces. I helped Maria to regain her confidence and move on with life. Stressful situations are encountered by us all. The loss of someone you love means you have to start all over again, but when you get back on your feet, you become much wiser and more resolute than before. This is often a better position to be in, than that of people who never faced challenging moments. Individuals who face challenges early in life tend to develop stronger emotional strengths than individuals who face such trials later in life.

The challenge before you Mark is to create a new dream, one greater than the one your father and mother had. You will need to keep searching for what you want till you find it. Nothing valuable in life comes on a silver platter. If you get anything on silver, platter you will never treasure it. This is because people place value on things they had to fight to obtain, and often people who inherit wealth lose it quickly than the wealth they build themselves. Ask the diamond miners, how many tonnes of earth they have to dig to get just one stone of value."

She continued, "Take a trip into the proverbial forest of your heart and search for your passion and pursue it. If you don't, you will choke in the dust of regret in your old age. Many people live in regret in their old age because they realise later that they never pursued things that they liked in their lives. They realised the folly of living life under the shadow of someone or living an artificial life.

To grow, you will need to develop your talent, and this takes time, and it may take you years to be good at something. The important thing is, once you identify it; work on it day and night.

No one comes to the Olympics without putting in hours of intense practice. Many people wish to join the race and win, but they don't have the discipline to put into perfecting their performance. Many people wish to improve their circumstances by doing something they are good at, but they dislike the hard work and sacrifices that come with it. Even talented people fail because of lack of discipline. Talent alone is not enough to succeed." Rose paused.

"When you are working on something that you are passionate about, at some stage a transition takes place, from one level to another and you will feel it in your heart. However, that doesn't mean you should rest on your laurels. Success is about conquering new heights and the new person you become after achieving your goals. It is never about what you get; it's not about the payoff. It's not about drifting along to the land of 'nowhere'. Unfortunately, no one ever drifts to stardom but rather to regret.

However, when you are working on your dream, remember that no matter how much effort you put in working on yourself, negative people will never appreciate your work and effort. Don't pay attention to them or try to get their approval. Even at high school, some students will disapprove what you wear, how you talk, how you walk or how you show respect to a teacher. You have to learn to live your life on your terms, and once you achieve that you will feel liberated. At your age, most young people tend to be too sensitive to what people say and think about them. When you get to my age, you won't care about what people say, and often you realised that no one was evening paying attention," said Rose.

"When I am on vacation, why should I read?" asked Mark. "I thought that is my time to rest and free my minds from books."

Rose drank another glass of water. "Many people don't

appreciate that you acquire knowledge and wisdom from reading books. Like anything planned, personal growth has to be intentional. A person desirous of knowledge will have to read books about his area of interest. No one accidentally becomes knowledgeable. The books of old tell us that 'he who seeks shall find', is that not so? Anyone who thinks he doesn't need to read is fooling himself. Everyone forgets with time, and it is necessary to refresh the memory regularly. Vacations offer a good opportunity to read slowly through all the material you went through during the semester; and also a time to reflect on what you are learning. It is a time to get help on topics that challenged you during the school term; when you didn't have a chance to examine them carefully because you were busy with other things. Catherine is three grades ahead of you. She will certainly help you if you have any questions. Always be prepared to take advantage of such opportunities whenever they arise."

"What books should I read to help me to know what to do when I grow up," asked Mark.

"There are many books in libraries, but before you read any one of them, you must first have reasons for reading. It is the outcome that determines the resources you need. If you want to be in business, you must read business books and if you want to be a doctor, like Catherine, you read medical books. You will need clarity of purpose to help you focus on a narrow area of knowledge. Trying to read everything you come across is not likely to help. Rather establish your target area of study and then focus on that. What you are best at and what your passion is; will help you identify your area of focus." Rose said.

"I would like to be a teacher, but I am shy and nervous when I speak in class. I struggle to keep my composure. When people look at me, I worry about the impression I am making; my voice, my pronunciation, my gestures and my selection of words. I sweat and my voice becomes shrill. I run short of breath," Mark replied.

Rose smiled and looked calmly at Mark, and she said in a low tone, "It is normal to feel that way. With practice, you will improve. Young people of your age tend to pay too much attention to what people think of them. If public speaking is your passion, you need to read books and articles on this subject and practise in private."

Suddenly a wind swept through the neighbourhood bringing with it dust and a change in temperature. "Let's go inside," said Rose as she pushed back her chair. "I feel exhausted today. I should have taken more time walking to and from the cemetery yesterday."

CHAPTER
16

Self –discovery and misconceptions challenged

For the next seven days, Rose and Mark discussed wide-ranging topics, including the relocation of Mark's parents from Roselle, Gabriel's successes in establishing a new life in Penrith, his death, the distribution of his estate and Maria's return to her parents in Casterbridge. She took Mark to the cemetery where Gabriel was buried. Rose's eloquence and soft-spoken demeanour touched Mark's, heart. The values she instilled in Mark in the short time they were together, made a lasting impression on him. Catherine also became an academic mentor to Mark and, her energy and passion inspired him to improve his academic performance and clarify his goals. She was well organised, dividing her time between her books, house chores and supervision of the children. She maintained her composure when her sisters knocked over a tray of dishes. Martha and Masculine felt thoroughly at home with Rose's grandchildren and every day was fun. If it were not for

Steps in the Middle

Catherine's reminders, the friends would have missed many meals.

Finally, Mark and his sisters' visit to Penrith came to an end. Mark was disappointed that he hadn't been able to meet Larry and Matilda, but the lessons he hoped to learn from them were delivered instead by Rose. Rose was indeed an excellent substitute for his grandparents. An emotional farewell on the day of their departure was lightened when Rose asked Martha and Masculine to select their favourite toys, which she carefully packed for them to take home. Rose hugged Mark as if that was the last time the two would see each other again. Her eyes were moist as she said, "Go well. Remember everything I told you. Nothing can stop you. Don't let anyone talk you out of your future! Your future is in your hands, every day when you woke up look at your hands, and go to work. You never be without."

Catherine waited for her turn with open arms, embraced Mark, Martha and Masculine. No one moved as if reluctant to part. Finally, Mark stepped away, followed by his sisters, and they proceeded down the street. They looked back and waved at Rose, Catherine, Doreen and Dorothy who were still standing at the gate. Rose walked back into the house and sat down on her favourite couch. Catherine followed and sat down next to Rose, taking her hand. "Don't be sad, Grandma," she said.

"I feel pity for those children. I was there when Gabriel was buried, and I was there when Larry was also buried. It is such a difficult thing to have children growing up without one of their parents," she said.

"But Grandma, haven't you taught Mark to grow up focusing on the future. You taught me the same, and I want to be a good coach like you," Catherine said.

"Catherine, you are my granddaughter, and I am happy to

teach you everything that I have learnt over the years. I teach you the way of life that leads to success and happiness, and the way of life that leads to sadness and pain. I have seen both worlds, some of my teachings come from experience; I have lived my lessons. It is sad for any parent to die, and not to see their children growing up. I am sure Gabriel would have wanted to be present in every moment of his children's lives. I am happy that none of my kids ever experienced what Gabriel's children are facing. I have done all I could to teach Mark about life in the short time I have had. I am grateful for the chance to contribute to his future," replied Rose.

Mark and his sister strode to the coach station, having had an enjoyable time away from home that they had been longing for. They looked forward to sharing their experiences with their friends on getting back. Mark contemplated the lessons he had learnt from Rose; that a child who grows up without resources but has hope will develop life skills faster than their counterparts with all the advantages of wealth. "You are responsible for your future," were the words that echoed in his mind and kept tormenting him. "Until now, I thought I was mum's responsibility to make me succeed and have a great future," he mused. Martha and Masculine were sad at leaving their friends behind but were consoled by the gift of toys which they would show their friends.

When the coach departed from Penrith, Martha and Masculine sat back in their seats, playing with their new-found toys. A child sitting on a different row kept looking at the toys, obviously envious. Her mother had a hard time restraining her from grabbing Masculine's toys until she moved her to a seat further away. Mark reassured his sisters that their toys were safe but even so, his sisters held tightly to the toys as if their life depended on it. "What is it about toys and children? Parents underestimate the impact toys have on children's lives. When I was young, I had a toy car made of wire which I pushed before me. It was fun," Mark thought.

As the journey progressed, his sisters fell asleep, with their toys held tightly on their laps. Several other passengers were dozing, and Mark closed his eyes to sleep as well, but he couldn't.

A week after Mark and his sisters had left for Penrith; Agnes's health took a turn for the worse. One morning, as she was on her way to visit Patrick's son who was down with a flu, Agnes felt dizzy and ran short of breath. She sweated heavily although she had only walked a few steps from home. She staggered as she tried to find somewhere to sit and soon she was down in a dead faint. A passing pedestrian came to her aid and called for an ambulance. Agnes was taken to the hospital, and for two days she remained in a coma. When she regained consciousness, she could not see or speak. The doctor who examined her explained that she had suffered a stroke which paralysed her body. After some days in the hospital, she regained partial sight of the right eye and subsequently the use of her right hand and leg. During the two weeks that she remained in hospital, her sons and daughters, brothers and sister and many church friends flooded her hospital room.

Finally, Agnes was discharged from hospital after showing significant signs of recovery and improved memory. The doctor explained that she was going to require full-time care by someone dedicated to her recovery. Sylvester, Agnes's eldest son, summoned his brothers and sisters to discuss options of looking after her. Prisca volunteered to quit her job so that she could look after Agnes, with the support of her brothers. Agnes was still not able to speak properly, and this caused her untold frustration, especially when she tried to talk to her grandchildren, and they couldn't understand her. Her lips and tongue were uncoordinated, and she struggled to eat.

Often Agnes would become obstinate and refuse to take food. Prisca had to stay awake at night looking after her and doing the best she could. The family was worried that Prisca would be unable to manage. Agnes tried on several occasions to get up and walk but every time she tried, she fell from the bed, and her face would be bruised. On seeing her injuries, some relatives accused Prisca of neglect. They blamed her for letting Agnes fall. One of Agnes's friends said, "Prisca, why don't you put her in a home where she would be looked after properly? Patrick and Conrad are wealthy business people; they have money to pay for whatever she wants."

Most people who visited Agnes during that time made their opinions based on what they saw during the moment they present, and only a few sincerely appreciated Prisca's efforts. Some people visited Agnes as often as they could; some only came once throughout her period of illness and some not at all.

Within weeks of looking after Agnes, Prisca became depressed. She was tired of helping her mother to bed, bathing her, feeding her, nursing her bruises and listening to what she was trying to say without much success. She also struggled to eat, losing weight much faster than anyone on a diet. She wished her mother would recover so that she could go back to work. Only after six months did it dawn upon her that Agnes's illness wasn't going to be over in a short time. Prisca felt like quitting and telling her brothers that she couldn't manage anymore, but each time she tried, something told her to hold back.

One day Agnes was lying in bed, trying to express something to Prisca who was next to her tidying the room. Agnes started crying when she couldn't get Prisca's attention. When Prisca saw tears running down her cheeks, she too began to cry, asking herself, "Mum, what have I done to you?" Martha and Masculine, who were outside the house, came in running when they heard Agnes cry. "What is it, Grandma?" Martha asked, looking at Agnes. Agnes was unable to answer, adding further to her frustration.

When the school holidays were over, Mark departed for Southwark, feeling exceedingly sorrowful for Agnes, but grateful that Prisca was there to take care of her. Earlier, Mark discussed Agnes's health condition with Dominic. "How do you feel about Agnes's illness?" Mark asked. Dominic replied, "I don't see any bright future for her. I am anxious about where are we going to go from here? Our lives are going to be tough." This conversation with Dominic worried Mark more than he could bear. He understood the vital role Agnes was playing in their lives.

Dominic went on in his usual pessimism. "The poor will always be poor, even if someone tries to shelter them. Poverty will follow them in hiding and chase them from the hands of their protectors. Agnes has been sheltering us but now our shelter is being removed, and poverty has caught up with us once again. We thought we were hiding under her wing as it were. There is no hope for us anymore. I wonder why the Creator takes away the good people and leaves all the troublemakers behind."

Mark put on a brave face and said "she will be all right as I see it. She is beginning to talk again. The doctor said she would need time to recover. Hopefully, when I come back from school, she will be walking again."

"Mark, it doesn't help to pretend everything is all right when it isn't. We have already lost Grandma. She might not be alive when you come back from school next time. There are two groups of people who were created; one will be poor and the other rich. No matter what the former group does, they will never succeed. I am in that category. Whatever I lay my hands on will not succeed. If I sow seeds in the field, birds and busy bugs will dig them up and eat them, no seed will even germinates. If I start a business either the stock will be stolen, or no one will buy from me, and I'll lose all my money. Recently, I went to a lunch party, and the waiter served everyone until it was my turn and she said to me, 'Sir, you will have to wait for your food a little longer; we have run out of chicken.' I asked, 'How come I am the only one without food?' The waiter only said, 'I am sorry,' and so all the people who were with me ate while I watched." Dominic shook his head.

"The second group," he went on, "are the rich who are blessed by the Creator. If you are in this group, you will always have the poor ministering to you. People feel compelled to give them attention. One day I went with Patrick to Southwark, where he was collecting goods he had ordered for his shop. I helped him to load the goods in the truck so that we could be on our way back as quickly as possible. The manager of the firm called Patrick and offered him a cup of coffee in his office, yet I was there standing and sorely in need of a cup of coffee. I waited to be called to join them but without success. I was angry because the manager saw me helping his staff but never extended the same hospitality to me. Since we are not in the wealthy group, we're going to be left exposed soon. Everyone's life is pre-determined by the Creator. You can't change your destiny. You will remain poor until you die. I have tried everything in my life to make things better, but nothing has worked," Dominic concluded bitterly.

Mark considered Dominic's words. He resolved not to listen

Steps in the Middle

to Dominic's view of the future. If Dominic meant that both of them were destined to be poor people, who could do nothing to change their fate, then Rose's words echoing in his ears; 'You are responsible for you own life,' were a lie. Mark believed in Rose's words, that hard work will help him to achieve his goal. His previous school records were a good example. He was determined to be the first wealthy and famous person in his family regardless of Dominic's predictions. Mark didn't want to confront his Dominic about his predictions because he was older and had deep respect for him. Instead, he said, "No," and walked away, thinking, "My mother and sisters are looking forward to me turning the wheel of fortunes in our favour. I will do whatever it takes to make it work!"

He clenched his fists as if he was ready for a fight against the unknown world. Meanwhile, Dominic thought Mark was crying. He began to feel sorry for him because he saw Mark as a young man unable to understand the challenges of life.

A while later, Mark spread his books before him and began to study diligently. "My success has to come from reading these books. With or without Agnes, I have to grow up and change my life for the better. For too long we have endured the crushing pain of poverty, and I can't quit at this stage. If I quit, there won't be a reprieve, and therefore it is better to die trying than to die without a fight. If I fight back poverty, there will be hope of succeeding, but if do nothing, I won't get a reward for my pain and suffering," resolved Mark

Every day as he woke up, he made decisions with the future in mind, hoped and believed that he was getting closer to achieving his goals. He visualised living his life like a hunter who goes out in search of food to provide for his family. He adopted a routine for regular study. He communicated respectfully with people, young or old. He improved his vocabulary. He sought new friends with similar ambitions, who encouraged him in the realisation of his vision. He had already foresworn alcohol and tobacco, having observed students who started smoking and went on to indulge in harmful drugs and drinkers who went on to become alcoholics. He wrote down his personal rules. "I will keep updating them as I discover something new," he said to himself as he rested his back against the chair. The notebook in which he wrote his personal rules soon became full.

"I will never miss any class unless circumstances seriously threaten my life. My education shall propel me to achieve my goal of travelling all over the word. I will never be guilty of any misbehaviour at school or home. I will never mock any teacher or student. I will never be arrested for any offence. I will respect everyone in my community including the authorities. I will never accept that a particular course of study is too difficult." Every weekend, he would allow one day for relaxation, listening to music and assisting Beauty with her house chores.

"I am glad I don't have many friends. Some students spend time with too many friends, enjoying themselves or trying to impress their colleagues or teachers with their beautiful clothes, money and careful grooming. My priority is to finish school and find a job and look after my family," he spoke to himself.

CHAPTER 17

Love, dedication and self-sacrifice

Agnes's illness prevailed, and months after her stroke, she was still unable to talk properly. Her left side of the body was still completely paralysed. She couldn't sit upright in her bed. She had difficulty in swallowing food, moving her head and other seemingly simple body movements. Responding to any stimuli remained a challenge, and she would sweat even when it was cold. Finally, she was taken back to Southwark hospital where a specialist could examine her. This was expensive, and Sylvester arranged for payment of all hospital bills.

From the time that Agnes was in the hospital, Prisca stayed with Sylvester's family in Southwark so she could be at Agnes's bedside every visiting hour. The hospital staff sometimes allowed her to stay overnight. All this was taking a toll on Prisca's health. When Sylvester talked to her about it, Prisca tried to brush it aside, but Sylvester persevered. "You are doing a great job, Prisca,

Steps in the Middle

and I appreciate your efforts. If you need anything, talk to me, and I will do whatever I can to make your task of looking after Agnes easier."

"Agnes's illness is not easy for me alone; sometimes she cries at night, and my heart sinks. She needs someone to feed her, and the nurses sometimes call me to assist them. Agnes is going to be released from the hospital soon, and I will be the only one to help her at home," Prisca said.

"I will hire someone to assist you as soon as she is released from the hospital," replied Sylvester.

Finally, her treatment began to take effect, and Agnes gradually regained movement, and the ability to speak. By the sixth month, Sylvester was notified by the doctors that Agnes could be discharged from the hospital to continue her recovery at home. Sylvester drove Agnes and Prisca, back to Casterbridge and Agnes' health continued to improve. She gained weight but was still unable to walk. She could utter some words, but she was barely audible. She also needed support to sit upright in her bed. Sylvester could not find anyone to assist Prisca right away, but some relatives came to her aid when they became concerned about Prisca's health. They came to help when it convenient, and as expected, they were particular with what they were willing to assist with.

After some weeks, Agnes developed bed sores that required her to change her sleeping positions regularly. Prisca had to be by her side every hour or so when she needed to move, and sometimes Prisca would also fall asleep. One night Prisca was in deep sleep when Agnes needed a drink of water. While attempting to reach out to the bedside table, she fell on the floor, and she cried out. Dominic, who was asleep in his bedroom, woke up and knocked on the door. Prisca also woke up and noticed that Agnes was lying on the floor in pain and the sight of Agnes suddenly shook her. Dominic opened the door, and on seeing that Agnes was on the floor, wrapped her in a blanket and lifted her up and put her back in the bed. In a rush to assist, Dominic had forgotten that Agnes had bed sores and the excruciating agony from these, coupled with the pain of falling from the bed caused Agnes to scream. She had injured her face in the fall and blood streamed from her nose.

Prisca went into a frenzy of trying to clean her up and position her properly in her bed. Prisca panicked and started running around the room as if someone was chasing her. Her heart was beating fast, and Dominic had a hard time calming her down.

From the day Agnes fell from the bed, she cried no more from her bed sores. Her reaction to any stimuli decreased substantially. Her sight deteriorated; she couldn't move her eyes from side to side. She stared in one direction for long periods with tears streaming down her face. It was not clear whether she was crying or she had a problem with her eyes, yet her face showed no emotion. From that day she never spoke again. She ate less and less, and feeding her became an uphill task.

Every morning, Prisca would move her outside to enjoy fresh air and bring her back before sunset. Then Agnes suffered another stroke which paralysed the remaining functional side of her body, and the situation turned grave. She started shivering violently. Prisca sent a message to Patrick, but he didn't respond. Prisca started crying while Martha and Masculine stood by helplessly by her side. When Dominic arrived from work, he was horrified to find his mother struggling with Agnes alone. He immediately called his uncles Sylvester, Benedict and Conrad, who promised to come the next day. The night was long for Prisca and Dominic, who stood by during Agnes's last moments. In the early hours of the morning, she quietly passed into the great darkness. Prisca and Dominic looked at each other in silent grief. As they sat next to Agnes's death bed, both of them felt relieved that her death had released her from pain and suffering.

Prisca questioned whether she had neglected Agnes in her last hours of need, by falling asleep at a crucial time. Had she stayed awake, perhaps Agnes wouldn't have fallen from her bed? Was she to blame for Agnes's death? Tears streamed down her face as she thought about all that had transpired since she left her job.

In the days that followed, people from all walks of life streamed to Agnes's house to pay their last respects and sign a book of condolences. Agnes's death drew more people than when she was alive. She had always led a quiet life away from the prying eyes of the public; even when her sons were successful businessmen in Casterbridge. Her sister, Aletta arranged for her burial. Mark came from Southwark along with Conrad's family to attend the funeral. On Sunday, after people had returned from the cemetery and just before they started to leave, Mark felt the void left by Agnes. It was only close relatives who were left when Sylvester called his brothers together for a meeting. Maria, who had arrived shortly before the burial, sat quietly next to Prisca. She was no stranger to loss as she tried to calm Prisca who had been crying throughout the funeral ceremony.

Sylvester and his brothers discussed some things while Maria and Prisca remained quiet. Their hearts and minds were in a different world. Indeed, men and women cope with grief differently. Maria was worried about her children while Prisca couldn't see a future without a job, she couldn't see how she was going to piece

Love, dedication and self-sacrifice

it together. They both wondered how they were going to make it without the support of Agnes. Prisca felt that the two years she had spent looking after Agnes were lost for nothing. She had no energy left to continue in what seemed like an empty life ahead of her. She fell deep into a depression. On the other hand, Maria worried about her children, couldn't figure how she was going to pull it off. Although Mark was now a lad, and Martha and Masculine were able to look after themselves, still Agnes had provided them with a comfortable home and was a generous grandma.

At their meeting, the brothers decided that Agnes's property would be transferred to Prisca and the children would continue to live in Agnes's house until they were ready to live. This was a great relief to Mark and his sisters.

After everyone had left, Prisca's disposition did not show any signs of improvement. She struggled with the trauma of witnessing Agnes's death. Her brothers, like the neighbours who visited Agnes whenever they could, did not understand what it meant to be with Agnes every day and night. Their knowledge and experience of Agnes illness mirrored that of a visitor, who momentarily gets emotionally involved upon sight of a bad experience and quickly forgets as they walk away from the scene. Indeed, it's one thing to be told of an experience and quite another to live it. After Agnes's death, all her brother moved on with their lives and returned to their families.

Prisca was left to pick up the pieces of what was left of her life. She found it difficult to talk about her experience to anyone because nobody had lived the experience with her, Martha and Masculine we still young to strengthen her. When Maria left for work, she decided that Prisca should be counselled by someone older and experienced. She could think of no one better than

Agnes's sister, Aletta. Aletta agreed to stay with Prisca for a week, but Prisca's full recovery would be difficult and take many years.

In the years that followed, Mark started living the ideas that Mr Wood and Rose Henderson had taught him. He had written them down so that he could study them and make them a part of his daily life. He made several amendments to the principles he had learnt and added some words and rephrases that made it easy for him to apply them. He would read the list of his life goals every night before going to sleep until he knew everything by heart like Catherine had told him.

When Mark finished high school with flying colours, his headmaster asked him, "What are your plans?" Mark replied, "I want to enrol with Oxford Brookes University next year." His time of staying with Conrad had now come to an end. Conrad congratulated him for his examination success. When he told him about his plans to enrol at Oxford Brookes University, which was also in Southwark, Conrad said, "If you need accommodation again, go rather to Sylvester and Benedict. Tell them that it is their turn to look after you."

Mark packed all his belongings, thanked Beauty and Conrad, and left for Casterbridge without responding to Conrad. When he arrived, he showed Prisca his certificate. Although she was unable to read neither nor understand the school certificate, she was nevertheless happy that he had passed his examinations. She said to him softly, "So what is next, what are you going to do now?"

"I want to study further at Oxford Brookes University. My headmaster was confident that I would be accepted at the university with my grades. Uncle Conrad told me that he would no longer offer me accommodation and that I should rather ask Benedict and Sylvester."

Prisca was enraged. "Is that what Conrad said? Benedict couldn't even look after his son, Bernard, in Southwark. Bernard had to complete high school living with Conrad, yet his father's house was a stone-throw away from Conrad's home. How will such a man be able to look after you when he failed to care for his son? Even if Benedict were to agree, what would his wife say? Will there be peace between them because of you?"

She had a point; Benedict was an incorrigible drunkard; he never missed a party where alcohol was served. He would spend much of his salary on drinking with his friends, even if that meant he had to walk home on foot. His wife and children struggled; barely aching a living in Casterbridge while he lived an extravagant life in Southwark. As an artisan, he was well paid and respected at work.

"As for Sylvester, he has a big house which can accommodate you, but I am not sure whether his wife will agree. Carol controls my brother and makes all the decisions. She talks too much. She complains about everything under the sun. She gossips with neighbours, and she doesn't like Sylvester's relatives. Perhaps there is no harm in trying. It's up to you! Maybe she will like you; you have to take the chance if she agrees," continued Prisca.

Sylvester lived in a more affluent suburb than Conrad, but Sylvester and Carol were already accommodating three grandsons. Sylvester was a retired ex-police commissioner. He ran a small transport company as well as a shop to keep him active. Carol thought it was time for the two of them to enjoy life in their retirement but unfortunately, their eldest son, George, passed on a few years before Sylvester's retirement. He and Carol assumed custody of George's two children, Gilbert and Anna. George had four siblings; Irene, Ida, Innocent and Sylvester Junior, known as

SJ. When George died, Innocent and his wife Megan moved to Southwark with their two children to live with his parents. SJ had just finished high school and was looking for employment opportunities in the industry.

Mark was doubtful that Sylvester's house would be the best place to stay while studying at university. He looked around for someone else who could to accommodate him for three years, but no one came to his mind. Maria, with her paltry income, wouldn't afford to rent an apartment while he was studying in Southwark.

Finally, Mark had no choice; he would have to ask Sylvester for help. Sylvester wasn't a regular in Casterbridge, and he hadn't visited in more than three months. When he finally visited Casterbridge, no one was expecting him, and his visit was going to be a few hours. Sylvester knocked on the door and walked in. Mark was busy in the garden behind the house. Prisca was seated on the same couch Agnes had always sat.

"I wasn't expecting you. Is everything all right?" she exclaimed as she rose from the couch.

"Everything is fine, Prisca, I was checking on my shop here in Casterbridge, and so I decided to come and see you before I return to Southwark." Martha and Masculine went into the kitchen and started preparing food for Sylvester. Mark walked in and sat quietly while the conversation between Prisca and Sylvester continued. He coughed to draw the latter's attention.

"How are lectures going at school?" asked Sylvester. He was not aware that Mark had finished school. Mark replied confidently, "I finished high school last year, and I passed very well. My intention is to enrol with Oxford Brookes University next year, and I meant to ask you if you could accommodate me in Southwark for three years while I study."

Mark held his breath while he waited for Sylvester's response. He wasn't sure whether that was the right time to ask him for assistance. He was afraid of being embarrassed in front of Prisca, and so he stopped talking and prepared for the worst to come. To his surprise, Sylvester responded rather thoughtfully and said, "Congratulations for successfully completing high school. I am sorry, I didn't know that you had finished. I am very proud of your achievement. Were you not staying with Conrad until now?"

"Yes I was, but Uncle Conrad told me to ask for help from you and Benedict, and if both of you can't help me with accommodation then I should come back and stay with him," replied Mark. Prisca sat on her couch tongue-tied; she was worried that Mark would tell Sylvester all she had said about his wife. She couldn't wait for Mark to finish talking to Sylvester and change the subject. Sylvester said, "Did Conrad say that? Anyway, I will go back and discuss with Carol, and once we have made a decision, I will advise you." Sylvester's answer came as no surprise to Prisca, who knew very well that Sylvester's decision-making process largely depended on Carol's views on the matter. Prisca perceived a man who always consults his wife for everything as weak and submissive. "Men should always be able to make decisions on the spot," she thought as she twitched her mouth and eyelids fluttered.

Sylvester left Casterbridge before evening without giving a specific date on which he would give Mark a firm answer. Days turned into weeks without a reply, and the first semester at Oxford Brookes came and passed, and Mark was still not enrolled. He went to the University to enquire after residential accommodation which was available, but a down payment was required. Maria couldn't afford the huge down payment. For months, Mark pondered what his future would be without education. Once again finance had prevented him from progressing to the next stage of his life. This reminded him of how he had once thought that it was too difficult for a fatherless boy to succeed. Now his goal was to break the ceiling of poverty hanging over his head. "Break it I will," he declared. "Then I will leave a legacy. I won't live hand to mouth or will any of my family ever again. I may be defeated, but I won't abandon my plans, this is a just a delay and I will be back on course again in a while. I will knock on the door of life with a new plan soon," Mark wiped tears from his face.

More time passed without a word from Sylvester. The enrolment dates for the second semester at Oxford Brookes came and passed. Chance and Phineas had joined colleges of their choice and were pursuing courses their parents had advised them. Mark started looking for a job to pass the time. He applied for many positions without success. He tried cold calling, but nothing materialised. Then Carol suddenly arrived in Casterbridge much to his excitement. He waited eagerly to hear whether they had agreed to accommodate him, but when he broached the subject, to his disappointment, Carol claimed total ignorance of ever hearing about it from Sylvester. She expressed sympathy that he had missed out while waiting for their decision, promising that she would discuss the matter with Sylvester and advise him promptly of their decision. Again, three months passed with no word from Sylvester and Carol. Mark's dream seemed to have come to nothing; the wait appeared to be a waste of time.

It was now a year after Agnes' death when the families gathered at Casterbridge for a commemoration. As was his custom, Sylvester called for a meeting of his brothers at the end of the ceremony. When the matter of Maria's children came up for discussion, Conrad asked him why he had not yet agreed to provide

Mark with accommodation. He went further to explain how the delay had caused Mark to miss university that year. He proceeded to challenge Sylvester, in front of everyone, to make a decision that day before sunset.

"If you say you cannot, then you must give us the reasons why. I looked after Mark in Southwark for five years, and you should be willing to do the same for a lesser period. Mark is your nephew, just as he is mine. I don't see why you should have taken a year to make a decision to accommodate him or not. In the meeting in Penrith, you promised Maria that you would help to look after the children. I am calling on you to demonstrate that commitment today," Conrad paused and waited for Sylvester to respond. There was silence in the house for a moment, and everyone dropped their heads.

The meeting adjourned to allow Sylvester and Carol to discuss the matter privately outside. Conrad's challenge gave them no option; they could no longer refuse to look after Mark or delay their decision. After a brief moment outside, Sylvester and Carol entered the house again, announcing that they were willing to provide Mark with accommodation for the entire duration of his university studies.

"I am very sorry that we have taken long to discuss this matter and I am aware that it has caused challenges for Mark. He has already lost one year which he cannot recover," said Sylvester. Carol was visibly unhappy, and although she confirmed the decision they had made outside, her facial expression told a different story. With everyone focusing on the decision they had announced, rather than her mood, the meeting progressed with its agenda. Mark, who was the subject of a discussion for a little while, was not in the room. He was in the kitchen helping Martha and Masculine prepare dinner for his uncles and their families. Mark's heart leapt with joy on hearing the news. He missed out on all the drama that played out in the meeting room, and when his uncles left, Prisca gave him the low-down. Mark was worried that he would be a divisive figure in the family. The last thing he wanted was for his uncles to clash because of his quest for education.

"Should I take residence with Sylvester's family? What do you think?" he asked Prisca.

"It is up to you. You are the one in need. He who has a runny tummy is the one to fight with the door to the restroom; no one opens the door for him. If you are afraid of taking what you asked for, Sylvester will come back and say 'I gave you a chance and you refused to take it'. You can't tell Sylvester that you were afraid that Carol wouldn't be happy living with you. It is not going to be comfortable living with Carol and her family; I know that. She didn't look happy when Sylvester announced the decision in the meeting, and she won't be happy when you live with her either. You asked for help, and they offered to help you in front of everyone. I think you have to take it since there is no going back now. Opportunity sometimes comes wrapped in thorns and thistles, and not on a silver platter."

Mark remained silent for a moment before saying "Yes, I will take the offer. If I don't take this offer, I won't reach my goals. I know it is not going to be easy, but I will prepare myself mentally and emotionally to live with them until I finish my studies. I will take the leap of faith and grow my wings on my way up".

"Carol is very particular with cleanliness and hygiene, your cleanliness will never satisfy her," Said Prisca. "Her tongue doesn't rest in her mouth; she always has to have the last word. Always take her plastic smile with a grain of salt. You will learn her as soon as you get there. Keep your focus on why you came to live with her; avoid getting dragged into family feuds. Don't try to prove her wrong or teach her anything. She is older than you, if she needs to learn or change her perception about you, she will change voluntarily. It is not your job to change or interfere with any of her children's lives. Do everything above reproach. If she asks for your help, offer it gladly. When you speak to her in the morning, do so with a warm smile."

Mark was reminded of his first months at Conrad's house and all the challenges he experienced while living in Claremont. Mark was familiar with a similar lecture Agnes used to deliver to anyone leaving home.

Carol and Sylvester drove back to Southwark in silence, each dwelling on their thoughts of the meeting. Carol had opposed looking after Mark because she and Sylvester had looked after Sylvester's siblings, Conrad, Benedict and Patrick, during their earlier years. She reckoned these three had a duty to show appreciation for what she had done then, by taking over some of the burdens from Sylvester. Carol was resentful of adding more people under her roof; she already had a 'full house'. Sylvester was now retired, depending on monthly pension payouts to make it from one month to another. She felt that the income from his small shop and transport business could be saved for a rainy day.

Sylvester, for his part, didn't favour a confrontational approach with his brothers. He felt that such an approach wouldn't be well received by Conrad, Benedict and Patrick. He also didn't want to be perceived as evading responsibilities, by using what he had done for Conrad years earlier, as leverage against him. He remembered the pledge of commitment he had made to support Maria and her children after Gabriel's death. He had assured Larry that he would do whatever was within his means to support Maria. Sylvester saw the request as an opportunity in which he could make a difference in the life of Mark, rather than reason with his brothers why he shouldn't take over the responsibility. At the same time, his integrity lay in him upholding his word, and he was ready to show that he was a man of integrity in front of his brothers. Carol couldn't sit quietly anymore, but Sylvester wouldn't be drawn into talking. He remained dead silent knowing he had twisted Carol's arms into accepting the decision. She had wanted to ask Conrad to provide accommodation to Mark for another three years.

Chapter

18

One option is left, it's painful and there is no choice

Mark was jubilant when he packed his bag before leaving for Southwark. He had hugged Dominic before he left for work. He did the same with his sisters before walking into Prisca's embrace. "Remember everything I told you," she said. "You will be all right; I have every confidence in you." Prisca patted Mark's shoulder. He nodded his head in agreement, picked up his bag and departed down the street. When he reached the bus station, Mr Wood was also waiting for his ride to Southwark. Mark was happy to meet Mr Wood as he always had.

"Who are you?" Mr Wood enquired. Mr Wood appeared unable to recognise Mark each time the two met.

"My name is Mark, Maria's son," replied Mark with a smile.

"Hello, Mark! How have you been? I haven't seen you for long."

"I came to your house the other day, and I heard you were in Southwark," replied Mark.

"Yes, I had gone to get a specialist examination of my eyes; my sight is failing me. Now I am going back again, but it is getting better than before. Is that where you are going?" he asked.

"Yes, I am due to enrol at Oxford Brookes University next week, and I am going early to get acquainted with the process in advance."

"I thought you were at university already. Anyway, I have confidence in you; you will make it," Mr Wood replied. The two sat next to each other and Mark revealed that he was going to stay with his uncle's family and that he was worried because he had never lived with them before.

Mr Wood urged him saying, "What do you think your uncle's family will do? They may not like you for a week or so, but soon they will get used to you, and you will get used to them also. You will be uncomfortable for a short while, and soon you will forget as you begin to focus on your studies. Don't worry so much about them, focus on what you want to achieve and if you don't focus your attention on them, you will soon find that your fear will begin to diminish. In any event, it's all right to be worried because that makes you concentrate on what you are afraid of."

Soon the bus arrived at Cranbourne, and Mark bade farewell to Mr Wood as he alighted from the bus. He strapped his bag on his back and took from his pocket the paper on which he had written Sylvester's home address. He had never been in Cranbourne, and as he walked from the bus station, he noticed that the houses in Cranbourne were grander than those in Claremont. Each house was built on a large plot with lush gardens behind high walls and imposing gates. Children had plenty of space to play. It was a more affluent community, and its inhabitants drove expensive cars. He was the only person walking in the leafy suburb. His footsteps echoed in the general silence of the tree-lined streets.

Mark was not sure where to find Jessop road. He was not quick enough to draw the attention of two boys who cycled past him; and as they entered a large property, the gate opened automatically and swallowed them inside. Then, he came to a bus stop where a map of the surrounding area was displayed, and on examining it, he discovered that he was walking in the opposite direction from Jessop road. After half an hour walking back, Mark finally rang the bell at Sylvester's house.

"Hello, what can I do for you?" Replied a female voice on the intercom.

"I am Mark, Sylvester's nephew," replied Mark.

"Hold on," came the reply. The person on the other end could be heard talking in the background. "Someone called Mark is at the gate. Do you know who he is?"

"I don't know anyone with such a name. What does he want?"

The intercom went dead without any further conversation. Mark contemplated his next action. "Should I ring the bell again or is someone coming to the gate?" he asked himself. He wondered if he was at the right place and for a moment he checked the address he had written again. He heard children's voices from behind the wall. Across the street was a tennis club where a small crowd of onlookers was watching the players. He pressed the intercom again, and this time he recognised Carol's voice. The gate opened, and Mark entered. Carol was seated on a chair on the patio.

"Mark! I wasn't expecting you today. Aren't colleges opening next week?" she exclaimed.

"Yes, I came early so that I can familiarise myself with the registration process before classes start," he replied.

"Oh well, here you are." Carol sounded unwelcome. "How did

you find this place? Did someone drive you to the gate?" she asked.

"No, not at all! I came alone from Casterbridge," replied Mark surprised by Carol's question.

Mark eased the heavy bag from his back and lowered it to the ground. He waited expectantly for Carol to offer him a seat. He noticed her cats were occupying the vacant chairs on the patio. Should he dislodge one cat and sit down? Would that annoy Carol? Many questions ran through Mark's head as he waited for Carol to offer him a seat. Carol's eyes remained fixed on her magazine for a while. Mark heard the quiet snoring of the cats and the ice tinkling in Carol's glass. The children playing with their bikes took no notice of the visitor. Carol looked up from her magazine, sipped from the glass, yawned and stretched her arms.

"Why are you still standing there?" She asked "Go and put your bag in that room. You will share the room with Sylvester Junior. We call him SJ. I will introduce you to him when he comes back. So how long is your course?" asked Carol.

"It's a three-year course," replied Mark.

"Oh my god!" she exclaimed again. So you want to stay with us for three years? Why did you choose a course that takes so long to complete?" she frowned. Her face looked like she had accidentally swallowed a snake.

"That is the way the course is structured; some degrees are even four years," replied Mark hoping Carol would be impressed.

"Are there no other good colleges in Casterbridge, so that you don't have to come this far?" Carol looked at Mark disdainfully.

Suddenly a man's voice shouted from behind the house "Gilbert! Don't do that. You will damage the bicycle," echoed the voice. Carol's mood changed immediately; she sprang from her seat, grabbed Mark's bag and led him inside. Suddenly, all the cats woke up from sleep and came after her. "This is our living room, the kitchen is here, and the bathrooms are on that side. Our bedroom is that one. Sit down here while I make some tea for you."

Carol switched on the television and hastened to the kitchen. "Do you take coffee or tea?" She called.

"Tea, milk and sugar," replied Mark.

A few moments later, Sylvester walked in. "Welcome, Mark! It's good to see you. You must have arrived just now."

"Yes, he had just arrived a few minutes ago," Carol interjected, as she brought Mark some tea on a tray. "You're early," she said looking at Sylvester.

"I was renewing my vehicle licence, and it didn't take long. Now there's a counter for senior citizens, and I was served in no time," replied Sylvester.

He turned to Mark; and with a friendly voice, he said "I want you to be successful, Mark; don't neglect your studies. You have an opportunity of a lifetime to improve your life. Nothing was ever achieved without taking the bull by the horns. Maria is working hard to give you this opportunity that she never had, and therefore once you are registered sink your head in the sand, make sure you are damn good at your studies. Victory will certainly be on your side one day if you focus. Make her proud. If there is anything you need from Carol or me during your stay, tell us. We want to help you achieve your dream," said Sylvester.

"I don't think he will need anything, but if there is, tell me first," said Carol. "I am always at home." Carol sat next to Mark listening attentively to the conversation between Mark and Sylvester. Mark said nothing about Carol's behaviour moments earlier.

Two of the children living with them at the house, Gilbert and Anna, were Sylvester and Carol's grandchildren. Their eldest son

George had fathered them with Sophie. But when he wanted to marry Sophie his parents considered the woman to be unsuitable and had refused to accept her as George's wife. They rejected any effort she made to find an amicable solution with them; they liked Sophie's children but couldn't stand the sight of her. George, maddened by his parents' behaviour, committed suicide, leaving a detailed note of his reasons on the table next to his bed. Carol and Sylvester assumed custody of Gilbert and Anna from Sophie after a custody battle that widened the rift between them and Sophie.

The third grandson was Blessing, from their second son, Innocent and his wife, Megan. Megan did not see eye to eye with Carol; she avoided any regular contact with Carol whenever possible. Megan and Innocent lived in a flat on the same property.

SJ entered the house from the back door and went straight into his room to sleep. When evening came, Mark was introduced to the whole family except SJ. After dinner, Carol said, "Mark, if you're ready to sleep, you can go to the room I showed you this afternoon." She and Sylvester then disappeared into their room, and so did the other children. When Mark opened the door to his room, he saw SJ asleep. Mark took the other bed opposite, and soon he fell asleep.

Within a matter of days, the enrolment process was complete, and Mark was able to concentrate on his studies. His good marks from high school enabled him to get sponsorship for his education without too much difficulty. He was registered as a non-resident student, meaning he travelled to and from the university every day. Maria had given him money for his transport and stationery requirements before he left Casterbridge but when Mark started lectures, he realised that the amount wasn't going to last long. His sponsorship didn't cover non-academic costs, and he knew Maria would not be able to give him more money.

Mark was hesitant to ask for money from Sylvester, fearing that the request would attract an adverse reaction from Carol. He sat down one afternoon to work out his monthly budget. The only way to reduce costs was to walk to and from university every day instead of taking a bus. This would mean leaving home at least an hour earlier before Carol was ready with breakfast. He was reluctant to cook for himself because Carol complained about people taking food from the kitchen without her knowledge. She insisted on preparing food herself and having everyone eating at the same.

Mark left for the university on foot early every morning before Carol, and the rest of the family were awake. SJ, Innocent and Megan were aware of this but didn't seem concerned that he had to forego breakfast. He took a short cut to avoid walking alongside the bus route. He felt embarrassed when other students saw him walking to university and assume that he didn't have enough money for bus fare. As true as it was, he didn't disclose how he travelled to and from university to Sylvester because he knew he would have come to his aid and this would have put him at odds with Carol. As a pedestrian, he was at the mercy of the weather; rain, excessive heat in the summer and bitter cold in the winter. When conditions were too severe Mark took a bus ride, but he would resume walking as soon as the weather improved.

One day SJ was on the bus when he saw Mark walking back home. When he asked Mark why he wasn't taking the bus ride, Mark replied, "I don't have enough money for that at the moment. I have to make do with what I have." SJ looked at him scornfully and walked out of the room. From that day he treated him contemptuously until he left Cranbourne. He went out of his way to make Mark feel uncomfortable. He played his music loudly while Mark was busy studying his book. Mark kept his eyes on the book he was reading but was unable to concentrate.

Mark fought back his tears and refused to start an argument which he knew he wouldn't win. He declined to share cupboard space with Mark, and this meant Mark would have to wash, iron and fold his clothes, keeping them in his bag. SJ insisted that Mark should not touch anything in his room. He complained to Carol that Mark had moved his shoes. Carol spoke to Mark in a low tone and yet very forceful saying, "SJ belongs to this family, and this is his room, so you must keep your hands off his things. You must allow him to be free in his room. Is that clear?" Mark nodded in agreement, purporting to have understood exactly what Carol meant.

Carol pampered SJ. Being the last born, he was treated like a prince and showered with gifts boys of his age yearned for. He exploited his privileges in every possible way. One day he accused Mark of leaving the bathtub in a mess, but on that day Mark had left home without taking a bath because the water in the house was turned off. Mark didn't know how to activate the valve outside supplying water into the house, and so he left home without taking a bath. When Sylvester heard Mark's response, he remembered the morning when the taps didn't have running water, and he immediately dismissed the allegation. Carol expected Sylvester to fly into a rage. When this didn't happen, Carol herself became hot with anger. She schemed to make Mark unwelcome in her family, and therefore nearly every day she tried a new trick.

Next Carol made a cake which she meant for a particular occasion the following weekend. When SJ came home, he cut a slice and took it to his room. Later that day, Carol asked Gilbert for information on the missing piece of cake. Gilbert reported that Sj had cut a small piece of the cake. Carol couldn't believe that Sj was involved and so she preferred to blame Mark. When Mark arrived from his lectures, she confronted him in anger. Mark did not know what she was talking about, but after seeing the piece of cake left by SJ in his room, he tried to convince Carol that it had nothing to do with him. But she refused to listen to him.

On occasions when he returned from university, the room he shared with SJ would be locked, and he would have to wait for SJ to come back and open the room. Carol became aware that SJ was locking his room when she said, "Sorry, Mark! That is SJ's room. Perhaps, there is something he doesn't want you to touch." Mark would reply in a low voice and say, "I understand. I am happy to sit in the living room until he's back." However, Carol was scared that Sylvester would come home and question why the room was being locked. So at times, she would open the room to avoid drawing the attention of Sylvester.

Mark wanted to keep the room clean; as he was someone who had grown up in the rural town of Casterbridge where he was no stranger to house chores. But it was not possible to clean SJ's room because he was forbidden to touch anything. SJ grew up in the palm of his mother's hand; he had never made his bed, cleaned his room or washed his clothes. Carol had always done everything for him. When he finished school, he stayed at home undecided what he wanted to do. Meanwhile, he spent most of his time playing music, sleeping until midday and watching movies till late. He joined a music group, and at night he often slipped out of the house quietly to attend concerts without notifying anyone.

One early morning, Sylvester was awakened by the loud noise

of dogs barking outside. When he looked out through the window, he saw SJ climbing over the gate. With rage, he went out to meet Sj before he gave him a piece of his mind. Sj proceeded into his room quietly before disappearing from home for another two days. Sylvester asked Mark about the whereabouts of SJ; Mark simply didn't know anything since he never shared any information with him.

With time Mark began finding it difficult to touch anything in the house. Whenever anything went wrong in the house, Carol sought ways to attribute it to Mark. Even going into the kitchen became a challenge for Mark because Carol would break things and blame it on Mark. Every day Mark left for lectures on any empty stomach, and he would not even have a pre-packed lunch. Whenever a student invited him for lunch in the canteen, Mark would excuse himself saying he had already eaten and yet that wasn't true. Although he managed to spend mornings without taking breakfast, lunch times were a little more difficult. His stomach would burn the whole afternoon with hunger.

Mark refused to pity himself; instead, he kept on reaffirming his commitment to achieving his goals. Meanwhile, on his daily travels to and from university, he would come across examples of things his family needed to be comfortable. At times doubts would fill his mind, and he would ask himself, "How will I buy a house, own a car, start a business and later alone be able to help others given where my life is now? Here I have only one pair of shoes, a couple of shirts, I can't afford to rent my accommodation. I am just a 'nobody' and just but a number on the surface of the earth.

Has anyone ever done this? I have always heard of people in business going bankrupt, people renting a house or hiring a car?

What is so special about me that those before me couldn't figure out? Is this education worth walking to university every day in the cold, being so hungry the whole day or facing humiliation from Carol every day? Is this worth the effort? My best friends are my shoes; they know where I have been every day and heard all that I soliloquise, about along the way. Sometimes my tears fall on my shoes and wash away the dust. Is this the way life is supposed to be?"

Mark would banish his doubts. "I have no other alternative. I know I am on the right path to achieving my dream. I am the one responsible for turning fortunes in my favour. It is my responsibility, and no one else's; I am the first born. I can't pass it onto someone. I didn't come here to enjoy staying with Carol, and so I understand her discomfort. I have to utilise the chance she has given me. If I quit, I may never find a chance like that again. I am not going to throw it away. I am going to face whatever consequence the opportunity will bring, happiness or pain," said Mark.

Another voice would say to him, "Why don't you go back to Casterbridge, a small town where you belong? There you will find your fit, and you won't have to struggle for anything, as long as you do your best. Small towns have enough opportunities for their own; there you will never go without. If you continue in Southwark, you will never amount to anything, forget it. No one has ever tried this before. Why are you putting yourself through this pain? The pain is soon going to be unbearable, if you continue this way, be kind to yourself. Boys of your age are working in farms in Casterbridge and have a love of their families. You don't have to be treated this way, can't you see that you don't deserve this. Come back to your senses and make the right decisions, go back! Just go back to Casterbridge!"

Steps in the Middle

In response, another thought would counter saying, "My dream is bigger than Casterbridge. She can't contain me; that's why I am here. I am already is a pain, I will have to get the reward. I have already invested time, sacrificed money and effort to be here; it won't be fair if I hang the boots after coming all this far."

That night, when the two arrived home, Carol went into her bedroom without a word. For two weeks, nobody spoke about it until Irene; their eldest daughter came to visit. She had three children and lived in the affluent suburb of Highlands, northeast of Cranbourne. Carol had a good relationship with Irene, unlike the rest of her children. Whenever Irene had something troubling her, she would discuss it with her mother and vice versa.

Carol said, "I thought things would improve this year over last year, but it doesn't look like it's going to happen."

"Why do you say that, Mom?" asked Irene.

"We were in Casterbridge attending Agnes's memorial, and before we left, Conrad stood up and told the meeting that Mark needed help to go to university. He said he had looked after Mark for five years and he wanted us to take the baton from him. He said everyone should have a fair share in helping Mark, and I disagreed. I wanted to refuse blankly but Sylvester stopped me, and I fumed.

After a while, Sylvester and I went outside to discuss the matter. I told Sylvester that I looked after Patrick, Benedict and Conrad since they were in school until they started working. Now they want me to take care of their sister's child. That is not fair. I am looking after George's two children. Innocent and his family are here in my house, a family of four. Sylvester Junior is not working; how can I add another soul under my roof. I feel like I am being crucified. Sylvester refused to listen to me, but he chose to listen to his brothers, and he agreed." Carol paused and looked at Irene naturally expecting sympathy and Irene did not disappoint.

"I pity you, Mom. Your misery will be with you to your grave. Do you have space to put him when he arrives? Isn't that a temptation on your hands? Why can't he find a job rather than trouble retired people? You should have stood your ground and dismissed the request. Besides people from rural towns aren't usually clean; you will have to teach him the basics of hygiene." Like Carol, Irene was contemptuous of her father's siblings. She couldn't stand the sight of them, and she would walk away from the house whenever they visited. The last time Prisca visited Carol, both Irene and Sylvester Junior disappeared before she could sit down. Prisca wanted to know why they had gone out so promptly but Carol evaded the question. Prisca was embarrassed that none of Carol's children and grandsons greeted her. Later, Conrad related a similar story when he visited Carol's house, and so did Patrick and his wives. Prisca was concerned with Carol prejudices when Mark accepted the offer to move to Cranbourne.

CHAPTER 19

Step through painful moments- can't be hurried

A secret will always have a way of finding its way to the open. That is what happened to Megan. Megan and Innocent met in Headlands where Innocent was working as a policeman and Megan was employed as a school teacher at a junior school. After knowing each other for a while, Megan and Innocent became engaged and started a family, and they had two sons, Blessing and Harry. When George died, Innocent moved back to Southwark from Headlands to be near his parents. Megan tried to resist moving in with her in-laws because a few years earlier Carol had told her that she didn't like her. After a lot of persuasions, Innocent and Megan moved back to Southwark; she left her teaching job reluctantly to become a stay-at-home mother.

Within a short while, staying at home became taxing for her, it was the last thing Megan wanted, but for the sake of peace with Innocent, she sacrificed her personal happiness for the sake of love. She struggled to see herself living under the same roof with her mother-in-law. Megan viewed Carol as petty, patronising and indeed she treated her disdainfully. Whenever she could, Megan avoided coming in contact with Carol by missing family events. She would only visit when Innocent was by her side or when Carol was apparently not at home.

Carol's dislike of Megan increased when she first visited Megan's mother a few years earlier. Megan grew up in the suburb of Islington, twenty miles west of Cranbourne, in a relatively modest house. Her mother was a full-time stay-at-home mother, and her father worked in textile factories, west of Southwark. The inhabitants of Islington struggled with many social problems including illegal drugs, alcohol abuse and crime, yet many families in Islington lived happily.

Many people in Southwark knew the suburb of Islington for the wrong reasons. Carol had never been to Islington before, although she had heard about Islington and its crime stories. One day, Carol and Sylvester were in Islington to attend the funeral of Megan's father. When they arrived, there were many other people in attendance. They took seats near the priest who was giving the sermon, and when the priest finished his sermon, two women came and sat next to them. They began to talk to each other, pointing to people and children who were around the house. Carol overheard Megan's name being mentioned by one of the women saying, "Look at that girl over there! She is Megan's first child, the daughter she had when she was still in high school. She is now grown up tall and beautiful."

Carol interjected and asked the woman, "Are you saying that Megan has a grown-up child? I thought she was only married recently." The women responded, "Yes, this is the child she had when she was still in high school. This was before she found a job in Headlands where she was subsequently married to a man from the police service. I heard that they are still together and she has two children with that man. Yeah, she had an appalling start."

"Has the child been living with her grandparents here all this time?" asked Carol.

"No, the child lives with Megan's aunt in another suburb not far from here."

When Carol heard those words from the women, she couldn't wait for the funeral proceedings to finish. Carol motioned Sylvester to accompany her for a walk. Sylvester obliged, oblivious of what Carol had in mind. "Sylvester, Megan is a cheat! A real liar," Carol snapped.

"Calm down; we are at a funeral here! Can't this wait until we get home?" said Sylvester sensing the rising emotions in Carol's voice.

"I was listening to the two women sitting next to us; you saw me talking to them too. They told me that Megan had a child before she married Innocent, but she didn't disclose that to him. Look at that girl over there; that's Megan's first child. What will you say to Megan, tell me what you are going to say?" Carol spat out.

"Calm down, let us discuss the matter with Innocent and verify the truth. Besides, you don't know whether Innocent wasn't told before they married," replied Sylvester as he went back into the house. Carol remained outside as she observed two young women entering the house, weeping. Megan tried to console them as they entered the house and it was their weeping that stirred the heart of most people at the house including Carol. On seeing their weeping, Carol regained her composure and went back into the house and sat down.

Carol's discovery that Megan was a teenage mother, who misled them into believing that she was a virgin at the time Innocent married her, infuriated her. At the same time, it gave her the much-needed armour she needed her. From that moment, she sought every opportunity to persuade Innocent to end his relationship with Megan, but Innocent was steadfast. He threatened to commit suicide if ever she were to talk about it again.

Carol controlled her anger, feeling defeated and fearing that Innocent would indeed follow George's example. But Carol was not to be outdone, so she changed her tactics, she began waging a bitter war with Megan, in the hope that Innocent would change his mind and leave her. She treated Megan with contempt, passed disparaging remarks and ridiculed her in front of her children. She sought the support of Irene in the fight against Megan, and often Megan would overhear them discussing her. In the face of this onslaught, she retreated to her bedroom, spending most of her afternoons alone. She would send her son Blessing, to fetch things for her from the kitchen and other parts of the house, if she needed anything. Carol refused to talk to Megan or share a meal at the same table with her.

Megan was ashamed by her failure to admit to the birth of her first child. She tried to apologise for the embarrassment she had caused Innocent's parents. Sylvester accepted her confession, and so did Innocent, both were able to move on with life after her confession, but that was not the case with Carol. Megan struggled with Carol's hostility toward her until she decided to find a job so that she could be away from her during the day, and in the evening Innocent would be home to protect her.

It was during this time that Mark entered the scene. Carol diverted her aggression from Megan to Mark, giving much-needed respite to Megan. However, Megan's respite came the expense of Mark; she soon found herself feeling sympathy for Mark. Megan and Mark soon began looking after each other's backs, sharing information and supporting each other during stressful situations.

At Oxford Brookes University, Mark aligned himself with other students who were brilliant in school, and this helped him maintain his high standards. However, when some students from well-to-do families started flaunting their wealth in the form of clothing, jewellery and cars; Mark found himself looking for colleagues like him. Other students became members of the Oxford sporting team; some won awards in beauty contests, music, literature, poetry and academic studies. There were students with a taste for fashion and designer labels. There were also many who hailed from moderate and low-income families. It was an excellent mix, and Mark easily found friends similar to him. Oxford Brookes campus boasted an array of sports fields, canteens and auditoriums, creating every opportunity for student interaction.

Mark remained an excellent student, but he found studying at home to be a challenge because of distractions from SJ, Gilbert, Blessing and Harry, while Carol's whinges continued unabated. "I have to use my time in between lectures to study while I am at the campus because once I get home, I will not have a quiet place or a desk where I can study. Last night when I was reading, SJ entered the room and switched off the light, saying he needed to sleep. Alternatively, I will have to read in the park during weekends," Mark said to himself as he walked home from university.

When Mark was in his third year, Carol increased her attacks, and at times Innocent would come to his aid and try to calm his mother. "What has he done, Mother?" he asked.

"He has broken my dinner plates. Ask Gilbert," replied Carol.

"No, it's not him. Mark had just arrived from university a few minutes ago. He hasn't even been in the kitchen," replied Innocent.

"Who else can it be? People from rural towns are careless," said Carol. "Gilbert!" she called out. "Who broke the dinner plates?"

"Uncle SJ bumped into me when I was carrying the plates, and they all fell into pieces," replied Gilbert.

"No, it can't be SJ. He wasn't here. Gilbert, you are not speaking the truth," Carol insisted.

"Mother, I will buy you a new dinner plates tomorrow. It is not Mark who broke the dishes. Don't accuse him," Innocent spoke, facing up to Carol.

"You were not here, and you don't know Mark very well," Carol replied walking away.

Indeed, when someone hates you, they will hate your shadow too. It was the increasing number of confrontations with Carol which sup blood from Mark's veins. He sought solace in crying privately. He knew there was no way he could end his stay with Carol unscathed. Each day Carol assembled an arsenal of weapons aimed at him, many of her jabs sank deep in his heart and some by virtue of fortuitous events he escaped. Carol concealed all her fights with the helpless Mark from the sight of Innocent and Sylvester but, of all other people knew the truth of her heart and they tacitly worked against Mark to please her.

Mark felt safe at school than home; he knew the home was hell he wished to get over as quickly as possible. However, nature has a way of allowing someone to go through pain, and come out of it better off than before. It allows a person to go through pain only to remove the pain completely when the pain has lost its sting. There were indeed times when Mark felt he couldn't stand it anymore, his breaking point was reached, and quitting was within grasp, but Prisca's words kept him going one more day. He could hear her voice subconsciously telling him "give it more day, week or month. You shouldn't come back without a victory." It would be many days before he could get the chance to see Prisca again; she had become a surrogate mother for him since Maria was away at work. Her words were still stuck in his head, and he sought to please her on his return to Casterbridge.

The following weekend Mark did his laundry before leaving home. His entire wardrobe consisted of two pairs of trousers, five shirts, three tee-shirts and two pairs of shorts. In his final semester, he added another pair of pants and a long sleeved shirt, and by then his shirts had become diaphanous. A change of clothes was made possible when Innocent handed him down some of his unused garments. Mark welcomed Innocent's gesture, and for once he had enough clothes to end the week without doing laundry midweek. Most of the clothes were over-size, but they were relatively new compared to the rest of his clothes. Style and colour were out of the question; anything he received was welcome. In the winter months, Mark alternated between wearing a black jacket and a blue coat. Often when the mercury dropped further, he would wear both and that meant he could go for many days appearing not to change clothes. His shoes were not designed for all weather, but they were the only ones he had. On weekends, Mark wore flip flops, giving respite to the soles of his only pair of shoes and headed for Hillside Park.

The Hillside Park was a beautiful place to spend time, especially during spring when flowers were in bloom with bees flitting from one flower to another in search of nectar. Brightly coloured birds perched on trees in the park adding to the excitement in the park. As morning gave way to mid-day, the park filled up with

Steps in the Middle

families taking up prized picnic spots. Fathers and mothers played with their children, and the dogs too had a good time running up and down the park. Couples connected with each other and everyone who came to the park seemed happy and contended. Life seemed perfect for all the families in the park.

Mark crossed the road dividing Hillside and Cranbourne, entered the park and took up a position on the north corner of the park alone. He carried with him the books he needed to read for his assignments. He also wanted a respite from the unpleasant atmosphere at home. The park provided him with an excellent environment to calm down and reflect on his life. "Where am I going with my life? How long should I put up with the living conditions at Carol's house and why am I here? Is this the best option that I have taken?" These were some of the questions Mark kept asking himself time and again. Each time he went through the cycle of asking himself these questions, his mind kept coming back with the same answers. This strengthened his resolve to endure the daily struggles. He saw his character as being shaped by the daily trials in his life, and as he dealt with one challenge after another, his confidence and ability to endure became stronger.

At times, he needed reassurance from Prisca and Mr Wood, neither of whom he had seen for months. The pain of living with Carol and her family for another year was a huge sacrifice he knew he still had to make. "No soldiers have been crowned with a victory before the battle is won. It is only when victory is achieved that soldiers raise their flags, and medals of honour are bestowed upon them. A true soldier fights to the very end, even if it means receiving medals posthumously. I want to succeed; it will be a victory for my mother and sisters too."

In the park, Mark stopped crying, took his notebook and

documented his plans for the coming year. Now that he was in his final year he needed to be clear about what he was going to do after university. For three hours, he wrote down everything he could think of, even though he doubted that he could do some of the things he listed, such as travelling overseas. A thought came to mind, "How will you do that? You are a son of a domestic helper; you don't have the finances to take a flight to another place. How will you do that when you can even afford a decent pair of shoes? You have never been at the airport anyway; you don't even know anyone outside this country."

Another thought came to mind with an answer, "What separates you from those already on the plane is that they have achieved their ambitions and you are still working on yours. Keep on working on what you want; your turn will come." Mark concluded that his education was what would make the difference. He needed proper qualifications to launch him into a career of his choice and that he was on the right path to success.

In the distance, he could see people enjoying a picnic in the park. Suddenly he felt hunger pangs; he had not eaten well the whole week. The thought of going back home and facing Carol took away his appetite. On several occasions, Carol had prepared dinner and neglected to leave a portion for him. Once when Mark came back from university, Carol said, "Sorry, I forgot about you. Just make a cup of tea and go to sleep. I will remember you tomorrow". Mark did as instructed and then went to his room. He could hear Carol laughing sarcastically behind him. She didn't believe in what he was planning to achieve in his life. She often said that he wouldn't amount to anything. She suggested to him that after university he should consider selling cabbages on the streets of Casterbridge like his mother did years earlier.

Steps in the Middle

He was in a house with some people who didn't have respect for him. There was lots of food, but it was not freely available to him. Sylvester was well off, but the way he raised his family made it difficult for them to enjoy life. Everyone in his house was obsessed with something that took the joy out of the family. Sylvester and Innocent had totally different mindsets; they didn't agree most of the time. They were busy people who were rarely at home. Although both showed interest in Mark and spoke respectfully to him, those moments were few and far between.

While in the park, hunger and fatigue overwhelmed him and he fell asleep on his bench. He dreamt of flying to a distant country where a beautiful people welcomed him; where he would start a business and soon become a well-known entrepreneur. His name would spread to distant lands, and within a short space of time, he would bring his mother and sisters to stay with him in the beautiful house he had just bought. It overlooked the sea, and the children could easily walk down to the beach for a picnic. He saw himself involved in helping children facing the same childhood difficulties he had encountered in his life.

"Hey, wake up! It is late. You need to leave the park now," shouted the park security officer. The park was now deserted, and it was indeed quickly getting dark. Mark lifted himself from the bench feeling haggard and lethargic. He picked up his books, mustered his courage and headed home.

Carol's view of Mark began to change towards the final months of Mark's stay in Southwark. He was not sure why perhaps by that time Mark had stopped paying attention to Carol's jabs. Is it true that the sting of pain more is more intense if one keeps focusing on it? Somehow, Mark progressively stopped worrying about Carol. He stopped freezing at her threats. On the other hand,

Carol began to understand that Mark was going to graduate with a degree and therefore she began to urge Mark to persuade SJ to pursue university studies. It had been three years since SJ had completed high school and as days passed; his hope of pursuing further studies was fading.

Mark realised that Carol was worried about Sj rather than him, and she wanted to use him to encourage Sj to take up similar studies. Sj's initial plan was to take a gap year after which he would enrol with a university. During the gap year, he took several jobs but could not hold any of them for long. SJ began spending most of his time on entertainment, attending parties and concerts, and watching movies at home all day. He would frequently disappear from home without his parents' knowledge and come back after two or three days without explanation. This angered Sylvester, but on the other hand, Carol argued that SJ was still young and he needed time to discover himself. SJ resisted his father's attempts to lecture him on his life and avoided him as much as he could. The two barely saw eye to eye, whatever the reason, it was Sj who knew the truth. He avoids being at home when his father was at home and often when Sylvester sought him, Carol would quickly come to his defence.

Sylvester worked in the police service for most of his life. After graduating from the police academy at the young age of nineteen, he rose through the ranks to become the deputy police commissioner, at the time of his retirement. He deplored his son's conduct and was quite prepared to push him out of the house so he could start a new life away from them. Carol wanted to retain the attention that came with being always surrounded by her children. The contrast between Mark and SJ couldn't have been greater in Mark's final semester. Mark received high commendation and congratulations regarding his academic progress from Sylvester, Innocent and Idah. They realised that Mark would soon be faced with a broad range of opportunities for employment. When the future prospect for Mark was becoming more apparent, Carol's envy and guilt began to consume her. Mark remained calm and respectful, preferring to smile and maintain his silence.

As he edged toward the end of his studies, Mark began to see a glimmer of hope for his future; he began to believe that his academic achievements could change his life. Megan, who initially seemed indifferent to Mark, began to view Mark as someone who had conquered a thorny valley and was emerging out of it, bruised but victorious. She envied Mark for enduring distressful situations and not buckling under pressure. However, not everyone was happy with Mark's eminent success; some still had doubts because they never appreciated or expected him to succeed in anything. Like any other 'victors', he never tried to make it his job to convince every one of his achievement. The doubting 'Thomas' continued to proceed in doubt, and the perplexed remained perplexed as he marched on with his life.

When the graduation day came, Mark went to the University alone. Maria was not there, and neither was his uncle, nor his family was in attendance. This didn't surprise him since, after so many years of running his race alone, he had become accustomed to standing up for himself, and fighting his battles alone. There was no pomp and fun when he returned home. He brought back the graduation certificate showing that he had graduated with distinctions. His victory was public but lonely, and for a moment he felt empty. But he was proud of the person he had become more than the graduation certificate in his hand. He had triumphed over his most challenging weak moments; when life seemed to be descending into an abyss and times, he couldn't see the wood from the tree. He felt like he had walked the difficult valley alone and paid all he had to come out of it.

Later, he began to look back at his life and noticed that every time he fought for what he believed in, whether he had achieved or not, he had learnt something about himself. Every victory motivated him to stand up for what he believed in his heart. He felt that life was like a school, teaching him to handle exciting moments and to maintain a bright face in the valley when things went awry.

Carol said to him, "At last you are done. You can go out and look for a job now." She seemed relieved that Mark would be leaving Cranbourne soon and her family's life would soon get back to normal again. She looked at Mark in his graduation gown and for a moment felt guilty for her past behaviour. At the same time, she regretted that SJ did haven't taken the similar studies. When Mark packed his bag to leave for Casterbridge, Carol tried to make amends with Mark; she wanted reconciliation and forgiveness. Mark assured her that he hadn't taken any offence from her and that she didn't need to plead for mercy.

Despite all the assurances from Mark, Carol remained unease with feelings of guilty. As she stared at Mark, it was as if she was visualising past scenes of cruelty she had meted on him. She rumbled some words, and her voice became husky. Whatever was running through her mind, it was only herself who could explain. As for Mark, it was just a happy day, and finally, the past was behind him.

"You can come back to my house if ever you need accommodation in Southwark again. Go well; I will miss you," Carol sobbed. Mark watched her helplessly in disbelief. He had never thought the spiteful Carol would ever shade a tear for any reason in connection with his life, besides he had never seen Carol feeling sorry for him before. He embraced her, and suddenly she regained her composure, although still tearful. Carol's tears landed on his shirt, and Mark watched the tears until the shirt dried.

At that moment, SJ walked into the room. "Where did you get this gown from?" he asked. "Have you gotten your degree now?"

Immediately, he noticed that Carol was crying. "What is it, Mom, why are you crying? What happened? " he asked.

"I am just happy for Mark. I am not crying really," replied Carol, wiping her eyes with a tissue. "This is a lesson for you and me, SJ. None of you children studied to a degree level. Sylvester and I saved up for many years hoping that at least one of you would progress to university. We hoped to attend the graduation day of one of our children, but that day still has to come. Today, Mark's graduation is my consolation. Thank you, Mark, for graduating with a degree and showing my sons and daughters that which I have always longed for." Carol concluded embracing Mark again. Mark felt awkward at her remarks and embraced her anyway.

On hearing Carol's word, SJ was immediately upset. His face turned red before briskly walking into his bedroom and banging the door behind him. Carol stood up and disappeared into her bedroom. Mark was still standing alone in the kitchen when Sylvester walked in with a broad and flattering smile. His smile was refreshing to Mark who desperately needed someone to share his excitement.

"Hey, have you graduated today?" he asked, looking jubilant. Sylvester embraced Mark and patted him on his shoulder. "Oh! I am so happy for you. After three years, victory is now on your side. Patience and persistence have paid you off. This is what victory is about, working day and night on what you believe in. You have demonstrated that not just for yourself, but you have pioneered for others and left an example for them to follow. I am very proud of you. Why didn't you tell me that you were graduating today?" he asked.

"I gave the graduation notice to Carol the other day. So I thought you knew, but perhaps you didn't have time," replied Mark.

Carol emerged from her bedroom in a rush on hearing Sylvester's voice. "My apologies, Sylvester, I totally forgot to pass on the message," Carol said humbly. "Come and sit Sylvester, I'll make some coffee for you. You must be tired." She helped him take off his jacket and led him into the living room. As Carol whisked away Sylvester to the living room, Mark remained standing alone yet again before heading to his room. SJ had already walked out when he heard his father talking to Mark, as was his habit lately. Mark felt heavy at heart before walking away from the kitchen and taking a seat on his bed. Although some might put him on a pedestal because of what he had achieved, yet he would remain humble. Those who thought he would not amount to anything and would not finish university were proved wrong.

"I am holding this certificate and wearing the graduation gown, and yet the status of my family hasn't changed. I am not out of the woods yet. The battle is still on. I have merely shifted territory. I can't rest until my life is transformed and that is my ultimate goal. I will go to Casterbridge tomorrow and take a rest for a week before embarking on a job hunt." Mark looked at his certificate for a moment and saw a mere piece of paper in his hand, and nothing much. He noticed that neither the paper nor the graduation gown had changed him, but his victory came from the daily battles he had to fight, standing or falling. It was in the daily struggles that he had discovered the truth above himself. The struggles refined his focus and sharped his vision of his future. It was in the thick of things that he grew the most.

The next morning Mark woke up early, thanked Sylvester and Carol before leaving for Casterbridge. His bag was strapped on his back just as when he first arrived. SJ was not at home when Mark left, so he left a note thanking him for his generosity.

Chapter 20

The ascend from the valley

Mark arrived in Casterbridge and began to draft a plan of getting a job. He reasoned that the best prospect for getting a job would be in Southwark, but he didn't want to beg his uncles for accommodation again. "Let me get the job first, and then I can decide the next step. Mr Wood said 'go as far as you can see, when you get there you will always be able to see further. When I get a job, I can find someone to share a flat with until I can rent my own. With time I can rent a flat big enough to accommodate my mother and my sisters when they visit me." Mark smiled at the prospect and excitement of hosting his family.

The following week, Mark took a bus from Casterbridge to Southwark and back every morning. He spent every day making cold calls on companies in Southwark without success. After a week he was exhausted. His meagre savings fast dwindled, and soon he gave up breakfast and lunch. He was no stranger to

Steps in the Middle

hunger, and fortunately, he had become accustomed to going on with his life without complaining. He kept affirming his vision that time would come when he wouldn't have to struggle with food, accommodation and finances anymore. All he needed to do was to persist and stay focused in pursuing his goals.

One day, on one of his fruitless quests for a job in Southwark, he bumped into Idah. "Hey, are you still in Southwark? I thought you went back to Casterbridge. I heard that you graduated with flying colour recently, is that true?" Idah exclaimed excitedly.

"I want to find a job in Southwark," Mark replied. "I commute here every day. I've had a few interviews, but I am still waiting for feedback."

"Oh, what a hectic program? Why don't you stay with Sylvester and Carol instead of travelling such a long distance every day?" Idah asked sympathetically.

"I would like to, but I feel they did the best they could for me and I don't want to burden them any further. I want to leave them to rest and enjoy their retirement years," replied Mark forcing a smiling.

"A friend of mine called me last week; he is a manager at the Thomas Meikles supermarket chain. He is looking for someone hardworking and honest to work in a supermarket. I don't know whether you would be interested as it's a very junior job. Perhaps you can pass on the information to someone who is interested," said Idah.

Mark's heart leapt with excitement. Without hesitation, he took down the address, and he was on his way to the supermarket. To his delight, he was hired immediately. "Where do you live?" the manager asked.

"I live in Casterbridge; it is a small town forty miles from Southwark," Mark replied.

"I mean, what is your address in Southwark?"

"Sir, I don't have accommodation in Southwark. I can come in from Casterbridge every morning," replied Mark.

"Look, young man; you can't afford to be late for work. All supermarket staff on duty must start on time in the morning." The manager replied firmly, and for a moment the manager remained silent. "I have a large house, and if you want, I can give you accommodation for the first month. Once you get your first pay cheque, you can look for your accommodation. What do you think?"

"I would appreciate sir," replied Mark with a smile. He couldn't contain his excitement; at last, he had a job in Southwark and somewhere to live. He felt like a heavy load had been lifted from his shoulders.

The manager continued, "You will have a one-hour lunch break, and the supermarket provides tea and coffee in the restaurant throughout the day. After work, you can wait for me in the front of the shop, and we can go home together," he said.

Mark commenced work immediately with Thomas Meikles Supermarket as a general hand. At the end of the first week, he went back to Casterbridge and returned with a bag full of clothes. He took residence in Park Meadowlands east of Southwark. At the end of the month, Mark was paid his first salary, and he was able to find accommodation of his own.

As the months passed, Mark kept his eye on a job in keeping with his profession. He was rewarded when he was hired by one of the biggest insurance firms in Southwark, a huge step in his career. For months, he worked hard to familiarise himself with his new role and in a short time, he became adept at his work. His supervisor commended him to his superiors, and soon he became a valuable employee of the company. His increased influence in the firm brought with it improved perks and other privileges. Mark's lifestyle improved accordingly. From the one-room apartment, he moved to a full house in Hatfield, east of Southwark. His wardrobe became a vast array of outfits. Within two years, he was driving his car, and with his company perks he took time off to explore the world around him.

Every school vacation, Martha and Masculine looked forward to being with him in Southwark. Maria also had her bedroom in Mark house. Changes in Maria's life soon became apparent; her face glowed, and her confidence and hope of the future became brighter. Every month, Mark sent supplies and assisted his mother with money, and soon Mark's realised that the money he was sending to her was more than she was being paid in her role as a domestic helper. The time came when he could realise his ambition of providing a home for Maria.

"Mum, would you consider coming back home and taking a rest from work? I want to look after you, just as you looked after us when we were young. I am now a man, and I can do this. I will commit to giving you at least the same amount of money that you were being paid in addition to looking after you. I will pay all your bills when you come and live with me? I will care for my sisters too and help them with all their needs," said Mark looking worried because he wasn't sure Maria would agree to such an idea. She had been working for many years, and she wasn't due for retirement yet. Mark's request was sincere and thoughtful. He knew he was doing the right thing by asking Maria to stop working.

Maria was silent for a moment. It was as if she wasn't expecting the request; her mouth was wide open. Perhaps, she was surprised by how fast time had moved. Many questions ran through her mind. She wanted more time to think about the decision. The thought of relying on Mark, the little boy she had raised to look after her, seemed a 'big ask'. Maria breathed heavily before responding. She looked at Mark's face again, as if she was in doubt but she realised that he was very resolute.

"I need time to think through this decision, and will also talk to Aletta and my supervisor. Once I get all the information I need, I will make my decision and then inform you," replied Maria. She didn't seem enthusiastic about the idea; her face looked visibly uncomfortable with the idea. Understandably, St Columbus had provided a reliable source of income for many years and quitting her job was no easy option. Although she felt Mark was capable of looking after her, she couldn't envision being looked after and relinquishing her role as the sole provider of her family. It was as if she never expected the day to come and if ever, whether it would come while she was still employed.

For some reason, she seemed to think the day had come too soon. Although Maria's income had changed little over the many years, she was employed at St Columbus, and she trusted her source of income. Could she trust Mark to take over from her?

Maria pondered over the thought of living a long cherished career that gave her stable income for many years and the friends she had made along the way. As days turned into weeks, she came to the conclusion that she would bid farewell to the institution that had looked after her for many years. She was proud of working for St Columbus Orphanage; it had been her source of pride and achievement. Within a few weeks, Maria was under her son's roof with all her children comfortably in their new home.

Mark's achievements did not escape the notice of Carol. She seemed to have forgotten that she had congratulated him on his degree and wished him well. A few weeks after she heard that

Mark was working in the supermarket, Carol remarked, "That can't be true. Thomas Meikles in Southwark wouldn't hire people from rural towns. Idah you lied to me." Irene, who was present, nodded in agreement.

Idah replied. "It's true. I referred him to Thomas Meikles, and he was hired on the same day. The manager at Thomas Meikles later thanked me for recommending Mark. Mark has since left Thomas Meikles anyway and is now working for a big insurance firm. The people in that industry are on the look-out for graduates."

Idah reminded his mother that Mark had the qualifications for the position. "None of us has been able to match what he achieved yet we all had the opportunity. Mum, you only gave him accommodation and food. He only had a few clothes. He had to walk to university every day. We can't take away anything from his achievement by demeaning it. Dad told me that Mark came to thank him before he left. Mum, you did the best you could for him, didn't you?"

When Idah mentioned that Mark had bought his house, Irene exclaimed, "What! That can't be true. Who told you that? Don't listen to Idah; she's just making up stories. She is dreaming."

"Last week, Mark called me and thanked me for helping him kick-start his career in Southwark. He brought some flowers for me at work, and I was very happy to for him" replied Idah.

Irene passed a snide remark saying, "That is impossible! He must be cleaning offices; that is the only thing he can do. What does he know? He will never amount to anything; I will never believe you." Irene looked at her mum as if to seek approval.

When someone's life improves, often it becomes apparent to everyone, and even cynics get confused. Many people who had known Mark when he was young couldn't believe what he had become. Many people believed that biography determines destiny. Many people avoid associating with anyone going through a bad time, even if the situation would be temporary. They conclude that a person whose background had been difficult can only become worse. In like manner, when Marks' life was going through a slump, Carol made permanent conclusions that his life would in no way improve. And when Mark's life began to come out of the woods, she couldn't believe it. Envy replaced her disdain for Mark.

Life has breaking moments; at times difficulties appear to overwhelm one, and often some people end their lives along the way because they fail to find a way through the valley. Sometimes, people make a permanent decision to end their lives based on a temporary challenge, some look at the present circumstances and quickly conclude that they are doomed to fail, and fail to believe that circumstances could reverse in a few hours, days or months and in some instances, they could take years. No one has good enough vision to see very far from where they stand, but if they take the courage to reach the furthest their eyes can see, they will indeed always be able to see further.

One of the tragedies of life is that everyone feels comfortable living with certainty, yet life never gives guarantees. Like anyone walking through a dense bush, you won't always be able to see where you are going or where you are coming from until you get on the top of a hill. From the hilltop, you will always be able to look back and appreciate how far you came, and at the same time, understand what still lies ahead. In the journey of life, everyone has their share of valley moments, no one is immune, but what makes the difference in the journey of life is what you do in the middle of the valley, before you rise out of it. Your attitude and

Steps in the Middle

determination to go through the valley and grow through it, will determine how soon you will come of it or whether you will come out of it in the first place.

Your reasons 'why', you are responding to your challenges the way you are choosing to, will always be your rod to comfort you when pain and disappointment come your way. Those who have succeeded in life were not set to succeed from birth, but rather they adopted clarity of vision and purpose, a dedication to working on themselves, day and night to achieve their dream, a taking of personal responsibility for their rise or fall, a clear hope that tomorrow would be better than the present day and a determination to succeed no matter the circumstances. Which one are you? Life gives you back whatever you ask of it, depending on the price you are willing to pay for it.

Other titles by the same author
Set them up for success: A practical approach to managing your team

Published 2016

Contact the author: rupiza88@gmail.com

www.ingramcontent.com/pod-product-compliance
Lightning Source LLC
Chambersburg PA
CBHW070539010526
44118CB00012B/1172